All-New

Baseball
Brainteasers

Michael A. Morse

Sterling Publishing Co., Inc.
New York

Dedication

In memory of my grandfather, Ben Jones, who watched Ruth and Gehrig from the same seats where I watched Mattingly and Winfield, and who ultimately left New York for the love of a woman.

Library of Congress Cataloging-in-Publication Data

Morse, Michael A. (Michael Ari), 1969-
  All-new baseball brainteasers / Michael A. Morse.
      p. cm.
  Includes index.
  ISBN-13: 978-1-4027-3101-3
  ISBN-10: 1-4027-3101-9
  1. Baseball—United States—Anecdotes. I. Title.

GV873.M67 2007
796.357—dc22

                                                2006021270

10 9 8 7 6 5 4 3 2

Published by Sterling Publishing Co., Inc.
387 Park Avenue South, New York, NY 10016
© 2006 by Michael A. Morse
Distributed in Canada by Sterling Publishing
c/o Canadian Manda Group, 165 Dufferin Street
Toronto, Ontario, Canada M6K 3H6
Distributed in the United Kingdom by GMC Distribution Services
Castle Place, 166 High Street, Lewes, East Sussex, England BN7 1XU
Distributed in Australia by Capricorn Link (Australia) Pty. Ltd.
P.O. Box 704, Windsor, NSW 2756, Australia

Sterling ISBN-13: 978-1-4027-3101-3
        ISBN-10: 1-4027-3101-9

For information about custom editions, special sales, premium and
corporate purchases, please contact Sterling Special Sales
Department at 800-805-5489 or specialsales@sterlingpub.com.

Book design by Evan Johnston

"THESE TV PEOPLE GET THE UMPIRE'S JOBS COMPLETELY WRONG. UMPIRES ARE REQUIRED BY THE RULES TO SAY WHAT THEY THINK IS CORRECT, NOT WHAT WAS CORRECT."

—Professor Raymond Lyttleton, FRS

Acknowledgments

My thanks go to Dom Forker, the author of the first edition of *Baseball Brain Teasers*; to Peter Gordon, my old umpiring partner who put my name forward to write this edition and who made many helpful comments; to all my friends who have suggested strange plays to include (Mike Avila [Questions 4 and 10], A.J. Conley [Questions 26, 27, 28], Rob Hodgson [Questions 16 and 22], Molly Morse Limmer [Questions 13, 47, 48], Seth Limmer [Question 15], Matthew Martin [Question 31], Ed Morse [Questions 47, 48, 54], Greg Williams [Question 52]); the website yanksfansoxfan.com (Question 14); and finally to all those Major League managers and players who seem to have a limitless capacity to create unexpected situations that they themselves often do not understand.

Contents

Introduction

It was a warm September evening, and I was listening to my beloved Yankees on the car radio as they tried to pitch their way out of trouble. The situation was tense—the potential tying run on base, full count, two outs. A well-known radio announcer described the action in detail. Here's the wind-up, now the pitch, and it's a . . . foul tip! I pumped my fist and shouted for joy. Yes! The Yankees sweated that bullet and were in a great position to win the game.

But wait! The announcer said *foul tip*, but it turned out that what he meant was *tipped foul*. A foul ball. A foul tip is a batted ball that goes sharp and direct from the bat to the catcher's hands. On a *foul tip* with two strikes, the batter would have been charged with a strikeout and the half-inning would have ended. If the ball is merely *tipped foul*, then he remains at bat with another chance. As it happened, the batter soon reached base, and the Yankees fell behind and eventually lost. This wasn't the announcer's fault, but he did raise my hopes with his misspoken phrase.

This little story really captures the essence of this book. Baseball is one of America's best-loved sports, but there is widespread confusion—even ignorance—about the basic rules and terms of the game. To make matters worse, much of what we think is true—our "common knowledge"—is just plain wrong. Rules are misquoted, terms misunderstood, history misremembered. When rule-book illiteracy misleads an innocent radio listener like me, the result is heartbreak. But when the same phenomenon actually causes some team to lose a crucial game, it is pure comedy, to paraphrase Mel Brooks.

In this book, you can compete against real players and managers from every Major League team (even the Washington Nationals), testing your knowledge against theirs. Most baseball fans are used to disappointment—we expect the best hitters to fail about seventy percent of the time and the best pitchers to be unable to finish most of the games they start. But we also expect our heroes to have a basic understanding of the rules, which just might give them a competitive edge. Many of the professionals that appear in this book could have used a little refresher. In the meantime, we can have fun dissecting their mistakes.

Don't worry if you have never read the rule book, which is outdated, poorly organized, and is an incomplete account of how the game is actually officiated. The rules of baseball are not designed to be needlessly complicated. They are simply there to ensure that both teams get a fair chance. A little common sense can go a long way toward understanding the correct call. You may be surprised that you understand the spirit of the rules better than many players and managers, who get easily confused in the heat of competition.

ALL-NEW BASEBALL BRAINTEASERS

This is the second edition of *Baseball Brainteasers*, and the title says that it contains all new incidents. There are actually two exceptions to this (Back to Home and Pinball), which also appear in the first edition. I describe these plays slightly differently from the first edition, and I thought it was worth setting the record straight.

—MICHAEL A. MORSE

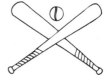

How to Use This Book

All-New Baseball Brain Teasers describes 60 challenging rules situations that have happened in real Major League games. (Admittedly, Question 51 is not very challenging, but the rest of them are!) Readers can test their knowledge of the rules and see if they can perform better than the professional players and managers who were involved in the plays.

Each incident is broken into three sections. The first section poses the quiz problem and describes the basic details of a challenging situation. The middle section recounts the real Major League game where the play happened. The third section explains the correct call.

The book can be read straight through as a series of entertaining incidents, or it can be used as a quiz. It can be read in any order, but it is organized by the type of rule involved in each play.

Readers who want to take the quiz should formulate their answers after reading the first section of each incident and before reading about the real Major League play. Answers are given at the end of the third section of each incident. Good luck!

1

Dead or Alive

Baseball is a sport without a clock, and theoretically there is no limit to how long a game might last. Yet, ironically, there is such a thing as a "timeout." At these times, the ball is "dead," or out of play. Other times, the ball is "alive." See if you can tell the difference between live and dead balls in the following unusual circumstances.

1. THE FALLEN

With runners on second and third and one out, the batter hits a foul pop near the third-base dugout. The third baseman makes a spectacular catch and then falls into the fenced-off area for photographers. The runner from third base tags up and scores. The runner from second tags up and tries to advance, but the third baseman recovers and manages to get the ball to a teammate, who tags the runner out at third.

Question 1: Is this a valid double play? Does the run count?

GAME Whenever the New York Yankees and Boston Red Sox meet late in the season, something interesting is bound to happen. In 1997, when the Baltimore Orioles had all but won the American League East, the Yankees were pursuing a wild card playoff berth and needed a victory against their biggest rivals. Trailing by one run in the sixth inning, the Yankees had Jorge Posada on second and Derek Jeter on third when Tim Raines came to bat.

Raines hit a foul pop that Boston's John Valentin caught before falling into the photographers' pit. Jeter scored and Posada was apparently thrown out at third base when Valentin flipped the ball to Nomar Garciaparra, who then threw to Jeff Frye, covering third.

The Red Sox left the field thinking the inning was over, but the umpires had ruled the ball dead the moment

3

Valentin fell. Jeter's game-tying run counted, and Posada was able to remain at third base. Wade Boggs then ended the threat against his former team when he also hit a foul pop.

The Yankees went on to win the game, 7–6, when Jeter singled home Paul O'Neill with two outs in the bottom of the ninth. New York eventually won the wild card, but lost in the playoffs to the Cleveland Indians.

CALL When a fielder falls into a dead ball area after catching the ball, the ball becomes dead. If he does this with runners on base, then each runner is awarded one base. In this case, Jeter was awarded home and Posada was awarded third. If a fielder enters the dugout after making a catch or goes in there and catches a fly ball, then the ball remains alive unless the fielder falls down, in which case the ball is dead and each runner gets one base.

Answer 1: It is not a double play. The run counts.

2. ROLL ON

A batter hits a high fly ball that falls, untouched, on the slope of the pitcher's mound and then rolls all the way across the third-base foul line, where it is picked up by the shortstop.

Question 2: Is the ball fair or foul?

GAME Batting for the San Francisco Giants in 1999, J.T. Snow hit this towering fly ball. The Atlanta Braves infielders could not agree on who would try to catch it, and they let it fall for an apparent base hit. When it continued its journey out of fair territory and finally met the glove of a fielder, its status became one of a foul ball. Snow soon hit another fly ball, but this one was caught for an out. The Braves won that day, 15–4.

CALL A ball does not become fair or foul until it stops, is touched by a person or other object, bounds past first or third base, or crosses into dead ball territory on a fly. The question is not where the ball has been, but where it is the moment it meets one of these four conditions. In our case, the ball was first touched in foul ground. Despite the unusual way it got there, it was a foul ball in exactly the same way as a ball hit straight back to the backstop.

Answer 2: Foul.

3. PITCHED

In the sport of cricket, to "pitch" the ball is to throw it in such a way that it hits the "pitch," which is the word the English use for the ground. In baseball, a pitch that hits the ground is not a very good one. But what happens if the batter forgets which sport he is playing and swings at such a delivery?

Question 3: If a batter swings and makes contact with a pitch after it has bounced, does the ball remain in play?

GAME Late in the 2005 season, the Philadelphia Phillies and Houston Astros were battling for the National League wild card. With the Phillies ahead by half a game, the Astros arrived in Philadelphia for a crucial series.

In the first game, Houston led 4–2, when Philadelphia mounted a comeback in the bottom of the ninth. After scoring one run, the Phillies had runners on second and third with two outs. The next at-bat meant everything. A hit would win the game and an out would lose it.

The batter was Endy Chavez. Houston pitcher Brad Lidge threw a slider that bounced in front of home plate. Chavez swung, made contact, and hit a foul ball. On the next pitch, Chavez struck out, and the game was over.

Houston took the wild card lead that day and ended the season one game ahead of Philadelphia. Chavez's at-bat effectively decided the outcome of the season for both teams. Houston went on to the World Series, but lost to the Chicago White Sox.

CALL Just as in cricket, there is no problem in baseball with hitting a pitch after it bounces. Chavez hit a foul ball. But had he put the ball in play, it would have been just like any other hit, and could even have been caught for an out.

Answer 3: Yes, the ball is in play.

4. BALL IN POCKET

The runner from third base breaks for home plate when a wild pitch gets away from the catcher. The ball lands in the umpire's pocket, and for a few seconds no one can find it— not even the umpire!

Question 4: Does the ball remain in play? If not, are the base runners allowed to advance?

GAME Houston Astro reliever Doug Henry threw this wild pitch during a comfortable 10–4 victory over the Chicago White Sox in 1998. Runner Ray Durham made it home while catcher Brad Ausmus thought about picking the pocket of umpire Gerry Davis. Even though Durham seemed to score easily on his own, the ball was considered out of play and Durham was awarded one base, meaning that his run counted anyway.

CALL When a ball gets stuck in an umpire's uniform, it is no different from a situation where the ball rolls into the dugout. It is out of play. On a thrown ball, runners are awarded two bases from the time of the throw. On a batted ball, it would be like a ground rule double (assuming that it was not umpire interference, which is what happens when the umpire prevents an infielder from making a play). In this case, however, it was a pitched ball. When pitched balls go out of play, the award is one base from the time of the pitch.

Answer 4: The ball is dead, and the runners are awarded one base.

5. NOT PLAYING THE BAG WELL

A runner leads off first base when the pitcher, with his pivot foot still in contact with the rubber, attempts a pick-off by throwing to the first baseman. But the ball glances off the first baseman's mitt and rolls into the dugout.

Question 5: How many bases is the runner awarded?

GAME The host Cincinnati Reds were trying to break a 2–2 tie against the Houston Astros in 2001, when Pokey Reese singled to start the eighth inning. Pitcher Octavio Dotel's attempt to keep Reese close to first base backfired when his pick-off throw got past Jeff Bagwell. The ball rolled out of play, and Reese was awarded second base. Did he eventually score to move Cincinnati into the lead? Read the next question to find out.

CALL On a pick-off attempt gone astray, the base award depends on the position of the pitcher's foot. If the pitcher throws while in contact with the rubber, then all runners are awarded one base. If the pitcher first steps off the rubber and then throws the ball, his overthrow would be treated the same as an overthrow by any other player and the award is two bases. This is not an arbitrary distinction, because the pitcher's position gives him different obligations, which I discuss in the next set of questions on balks.

Answer 5: One base.

The Balk

There is probably no more mysterious rule in baseball than the balk. Sometimes the ball remains alive, sometimes it is dead. Announcers often have a hard time explaining what happened. The following pages provide three examples to test your balk literacy.

6. NO TIME

With a runner on second base, the pitcher is in the set position, ready to make the next pitch. Just as he starts his windup, the batter asks for time. The umpire correctly refuses the request. But the pitcher becomes confused and halts his delivery.

Question 6: Is this a balk? The call is on page 18.

GAME In the same 2001 Cincinnati-Houston game from the previous question, and on the very play following the overthrow to first, Octavio Dotel failed to complete his pitch when he saw Reds batter Jason LaRue ask for time. After initially calling a balk, the umpires got together and decided to nullify the play. LaRue later popped out on a bunt for the first out of the half-inning.

Cincinnati manager Bob Boone threatened to protest the game over this decision, but it would not have made any difference. Pinch hitter Calvin Pickering hit a single that drove home Pokey Reese from second base. The Reds won the game, 3–2.

7. OOPS

In a scoreless game, the visitors have runners on first and third with two outs. As the pitcher assumes the set position, he loses concentration for a moment and drops the ball to the ground. Neither runner was moving.

Question 7: Is this a balk or, because the pitcher was standing on the rubber, is it called a "ball?" The call is on page 18.

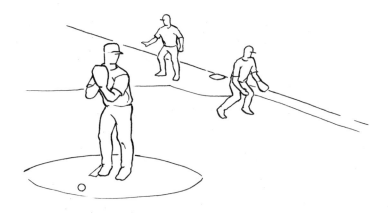

GAME Pitcher Kerry Wood of the Chicago Cubs was guilty of a costly dropped ball during a game against the Milwaukee Brewers in 2000. When the ball hit the ground, the umpires called a balk, scoring Ron Belliard from third base and moving Marquis Grissom to second base. Wood recovered and helped Chicago to a 4–2 victory.

8. FAKE-OUT

The score is tied 1–1 in the bottom of the 14th inning, and the home team has runners on first and third with one out. With no balls and two strikes on the batter, the pitcher believes that the runner from first will try to steal second, so he tries a pick-off move. The pitcher, using only his arm, fakes a throw to third base and then wheels around and steps and throws to first base.

Question 8: Is this a balk? The call is on page 18.

GAME Some say that baseball is like chess, not in the sense that it is incredibly slow and boring but because managers are often thinking several moves ahead. In this particular game in 2004, Oakland A's manager Ken Macha tried to be so clever that he called for a play that was of limited potential benefit and ended up costing his team the game.

The strangeness began in the ninth inning, when the host Seattle Mariners blew a 1–0 lead by giving up a home run to Oakland's Jermaine Dye. Dye's blast would have been caught by Seattle's Ichiro Suzuki, except that a fan got in the way. The game was tied 1–1.

Almost five hours since the game began, the Mariners were threatening to score in the 14th, with Bret Boone on first and Quinton McCracken on third and one out. A's pitcher Justin Duchscherer ran the count to 0–2 against Scott Spiezio.

In this situation, the Mariners had two priorities: score the runner from third and try to avoid a double-play that would end the inning. The A's, on the other hand, were looking for outs and were desperate to stop the runner on third from scoring. Macha thought he had figured out a sneaky way to get an out by anticipating Seattle's focus on avoiding a double play. With an 0–2 count, he called for a fake throw to third base and a quick return throw to first base.

There were two problems with the execution of the play, however. First, the pitcher did not step toward third base during his fake throw. Second, the first baseman was not aware of the plan and was standing well off of his base, making it impossible to record an out there whatever happened.

In this dazzling display of move and countermove, the A's neglected their main priority of stopping a run from scoring. The umpires called a balk, and the game ended there and then.

Duchscherer is only the latest in a long line of pitchers to have lost a game on a balk call. Others who have fallen victim to the so-called "balk-off" game-ending play are Matt Turner (causing the Florida Marlins to lose to the Atlanta Braves in 1993), Jeff Zimmerman (causing the Texas Rangers to lose to the Baltimore Orioles in 2000), and John Rocker (this time causing the Braves to lose to the Marlins in 2000).

CALL Here is not the place to describe the dozen-plus ways to balk. But by keeping in mind some basic ideas, you should be able to understand when a balk does or does not occur.

The balk is a penalty imposed when the defense gains an unfair advantage in deceiving a base runner through a violation of the rules, and it leads to a one-base award. This is a delayed dead ball, so that the offense is not penalized, if, for example, a batter hits a home run on an illegal pitch.

Most balk violations happen because a pitcher fails to do one of the three things he must do if he is standing on the rubber with runners on base: pitch the ball (following a complete stop with his hands together, if he is in the set position); step and throw to an occupied base (or, in the case of second and third bases, he can step and fake a throw); or step backwards off of the rubber while separating his hands. Failure to do one of these three things will result in a balk.

Once a pitcher steps off the rubber, he is free of these obligations and can do almost anything (except pitch or pretend to pitch). He can throw to an unoccupied base, fake a throw to first base, throw without stepping toward a base, drop the ball, and so forth.

Following these guidelines, two of the balk calls are obvious. When Wood dropped the ball, he did something that was not one of his three obligations. (Had he dropped the ball so wildly that it crossed a foul line, then it would have been considered a pitch and almost certainly a "ball.") Likewise, when Duchscherer faked to third base without stepping in that direction, he committed a balk.

Dotel's non-balk is not so clear, however. He also failed to perform one of the three obligations, but in his case it was not his fault, so the balk was not called. The rule book states that batters will not be granted time when a pitcher is in the set position or has started a delivery. If a batter steps out the box, then the pitch will count. To protect pitchers from batters who try to distract them, the rules also state that when a batter steps out of the box and cause a pitcher to balk, then both infractions will be ignored and the play will not count.

On Dotel's halted delivery, however, LaRue remained in the box, which is why Boone considered protesting the call. But the rules go further and say that no balk can be called when a member of the offensive team calls "time" for the purposes of trying to induce a balk. If the umpires thought that LaRue was purposefully trying to cause a balk, then they would have ejected him from the game. In this case, they decided that his deception was unintentional but still unfair to the pitcher. The umpires applied their common sense and nullified the play.

Here are the answers:

> 6. *No balk.*
> 7. *It's a balk.*
> 8. *It's a balk.*

9. A TIP FROM ME

This question is just to see if you're paying attention, because I have already given you the answer elsewhere in the book. There is a man on first base with no outs. The count on the batter is 3–2. On the next pitch, the runner is moving, the batter swings, and the umpire calls a foul tip.

Question 9: Is the batter out? Does the runner have to go back to first base?

GAME In 2005, the soon-to-be-crowned world champion Chicago White Sox were visiting the Toronto Blue Jays. Timo Pérez started the top of the second inning with a base hit off Blue Jay starter Dave Bush. The next batter, Jermaine Dye, had three balls and two strikes on him when Bush delivered the payoff pitch. Dye swung and just nicked the ball, which went directly into the mitt of catcher Gregg Zaun. This foul tip counts exactly the same as any swinging strike. Dye was out and Pérez swiped second base.

The next batter, A. J. Pierzynski, popped out to the second baseman, and Pérez was doubled off to end the inning. The White Sox eventually won the game, 5–3.

CALL I describe foul tips in the book's introduction, but it's worth repeating here: a foul tip, by definition, is caught by the catcher directly after it nicks the bat. It is counted as a strike, and the ball remains alive. If a batter swings and tips the ball foul (and it is not caught), it is a foul ball, not a foul tip. In our example, had there been fewer than two strikes when the foul tip occurred, then Dye would not have struck out.

Foul tip. Foul ball. Different things.

*Answer 9: **The batter is out, and the runner does not have to return to first base.***

Baseball Hurts

Professional athletes sometimes suffer for their life of glory and riches. No pain no gain, they say. What the following strange plays have in common is that a player or visiting animal had an unpleasant and highly unusual experience, creating a conundrum for the umpires.

10. JOHNSON VERSUS BIRD

A hard-throwing fastballer tries to whiz one past the batter when an unlucky bird comes in from behind the plate and takes the full impact of the pitch before the batter gets a chance to swing.

Question 10: Does the ball stay in play and does the pitch count?

GAME In the 1980s, the great rivalry in basketball was Magic Johnson versus Larry Bird. Baseball had its own Johnson versus bird match-up, but in this case the bird was a doomed dove. During a spring training game in 2001, Arizona Diamondback pitcher Randy Johnson threw a pitch that never reached its target, but was intercepted by a bird that gave its life for the sake of a strange rules anecdote. In the interest of fairness, the umpires ruled a "do-over" by calling a timeout and allowing Johnson to try the pitch again.

This seems like a once-in-a-lifetime play, but it happened again in 2006 in a minor league clash between the Buffalo Bisons and Durham Bulls. This time the bird was a seagull and it survived.

CALL Going by the letter of the rules, this pitch should have been called a ball with no runners on base or a balk if there had been runners. But in this case, the umpires exercised their discretion to rule on an incident that is not mentioned in the rule book, and they came up with a simple solution: a "do-over." The rule book mentions animals that get in the way of batted or thrown balls (see next question), but it has not yet been updated to account for pitched balls. It would be interesting to know what would happen if a wild pitch or passed ball hit a bird after the batter had a chance to swing. The umpires would probably allow play to continue in this case, but since it has never happened and is not covered by the rule book, we will have to wait and see.

Answer 10: No and no.

11. IN THE FLIGHT PATH

A batter hits a routine pop fly that deflects off of a bird. The ball, which probably would have been caught for an out, lands in the outfield, and the batter makes it to second base.

Question 11: Does the ball stay in play and does the hit count?

GAME In 1987, Dion James of the Atlanta Braves, batting against the New York Mets at Shea Stadium, benefited from the "sacrifice fly" of a bird that gave its life so that James could reach second base. The ball deflected off the unlucky bird and eluded outfielder Kevin McReynolds.

CALL Because this was a batted ball, rather than a pitched ball, the umpires let the play proceed as if nothing had happened. The "fan interference" rule only applies to ticket-paying humans. In cases of interference by birds or other animals (squirrels, cats, and mice come to mind), play usually continues. This makes sense once the batter has had a chance to hit the ball. The animal is, in a sense, part of the field of play, no different from a gust of wind or divot in the grass.

Answer 11: Yes and yes.

12. A SWING AND A HIT . . . BATSMAN

The home team is batting with the bases loaded in extra innings and the score tied. A one-out, two-strike pitch hits the batter, but the batter has already swung at it.

Question 12: Is the batter out or has his team just won the game or both?

GAME The unlucky batter in this case was Tom Goodwin of the Los Angeles Dodgers, facing San Diego Padre pitcher Jay Witasick in 2001. The score was tied, 6–6, in the 10th when the Dodgers, apparently on the verge of victory, loaded the bases with one out. When Goodwin swung at the pitch and missed, he was called out on strikes instead of getting a free ride to first base for being hit by the pitch. The play bruised his ego as well. San Diego survived the inning and went on to win the game in the 11th, 7–6.

CALL   There are two situations where a hit batsman is not awarded first base. The first is when the pitch is a strike, either because it hits the batter in the strike zone or because the batter swings and misses. The second case is when the umpire thinks that the batter could have gotten out of the way but chose to get hit on purpose. Sometimes this can be a difficult judgment call. Batters do not have to move in order to prove they are trying to avoid being plunked, because umpires understand that there is very little time to decide which way to turn away. If a pitch nicks a batter's uniform rather than the body, then it still counts as a hit batsman. In all of these cases, the ball is dead.

Answer 12: He's out. The ball is dead and no runner can advance.

13. OUCH

The batter hits a screaming line drive that smacks the pitcher directly in the face, seriously injuring him. While the pitcher is writhing in pain and in need of immediate medical attention, the ball rebounds all the way to the backstop.

Question 13: Is it an automatic timeout when a player is injured? If so, is the batter credited with a hit?

GAME In 2002, Los Angeles Dodger rookie pitcher Kazuhisa Ishii was victimized by a line drive off the bat of Brian Hunter of the Houston Astros. While paramedics ran out onto the field to help Ishii, the ball rolled to the backstop, and Hunter advanced to second base for a double that drove in a run. Ishii spent several days in the hospital with a small fracture in his skull and a concussion. He also had surgery to remove a chipped bone from his nasal passage. Houston won the contest 6–2, and Ishii was the losing pitcher.

While batters and base runners have the protection of helmets, pitchers remain vulnerable to hard hit baseballs that leave them almost no time to react and get out of the way. A few other pitchers have also sustained serious injuries in recent years, and it may not be long before an even more serious incident forces the Major Leagues to consider some form of protection for pitchers.

In 2003, Kevin Olsen of the Florida Marlins was lucky to have nothing more than six stitches, a concussion, and a one-night hospital stay after Todd Walker of the Boston Red

Sox hit a line drive off of his right ear. In 2000, pitcher Bryce Florie of the Red Sox was very seriously injured when Ryan Thompson of the New York Yankees hit a ball directly onto his eye. Florie bled profusely, had bone fractures in his face, and lost some of his vision. Although he tried to return to baseball the following season, that play effectively ended his career.

In all three of these cases, the pitcher who was hit in the head was also on the losing side.

CALL No matter how badly injured a player may be, the play will always continue in baseball. If a fielder is injured on a hit ball, the batter can continue running as if nothing has happened. The same is true when runners are injured. Many runners have been tagged out after falling victim to injuries while rounding the bases.

Answer 13: The ball stays alive, and the batter and any runners can advance as far as they are willing to go.

14. ACHILLES HEEL

With two men out and a runner on first base, the batter hits a home run over the left-field wall. But the lead runner collapses between second and third with a torn Achilles tendon and is unable to continue. The batter reaches second base and stops, unsure of what to do next.

Question 14: Does the lead runner's sudden injury mean he is out for abandoning his effort, thus ending the inning and nullifying the home run? Or is there some way that this apparent two-run home run can be completed?

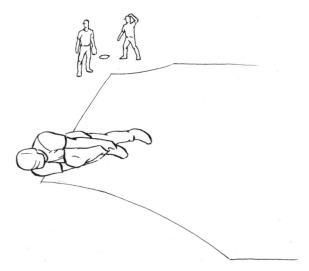

GAME The Boston Red Sox were north of the border in September 2005, battling the Toronto Blue Jays and trying to keep the division lead out of the hands of the resurgent New York Yankees. Gabe Kapler (who himself was playing in place of the injured Johnny Damon) fell facedown between second and third just as Tony Graffanino's blast over the fence seemed to give Boston a 3–2 lead. For a moment it looked like the runners would never complete their journey around the bases and that Toronto would instead preserve its 2–1 advantage.

Boston manager Terry Francona came out to tend to his player. When it was clear that Kapler would not be able to touch third base and home plate, Francona announced pinch-runner Alejandro Machado, who was able to complete the circuit and score his first-ever Major League run.

Francona's quick-thinking substitution proved decisive in giving Boston a 5–3 victory. This helped the Red Sox to keep the Yankees at bay—at least until the last weekend of the season when New York stole the division title. Both teams went to the playoffs and both lost in the first round.

CALL Substitutions are allowed at any time the ball is dead, allowing for certain caveats, for example about people in the starting lineup actually playing before they leave the game. When a home run has been hit over the fence, it is in dead-ball territory. The rule book specifically mentions cases where a player is injured like this, to make sure that teams know that they can bring in pinch runners to take bases that have already been awarded. It is a different story, however, if the ball is alive. In that case, Kapler's Achilles tendon might have been Boston's Achilles heel, so to speak.

Answer 14: The home run can be completed if the batting team substitutes for the injured player.

Knowing the Basics

Nine innings, nine batters, three outs, four bases. These are some of the basics of baseball. See if you understand them better than some of the pros.

15. AN "IDIOT" ON THE BASEPATHS

The runner on first base makes a dash for second with a 3–1 count on the batter. The pitch comes in as ball four. Meanwhile, the catcher makes the throw to second base just in case the pitch was called a strike. The runner slides into second ahead of the throw, but then steps off momentarily toward center field as the shortstop continues to hold the tag on him.

Question 15: Is the runner out or does he remain at second base because of the walk?

GAME Self-described "idiot" and speed-demon Johnny Damon of the Boston Red Sox was on the move during this pitch to

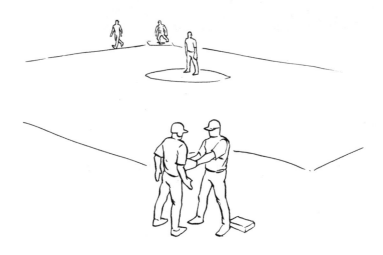

Trot Nixon by Tanyon Sturtze of the New York Yankees early in the 2005 season. On the walk, Damon had a free pass to second, but when he stepped past the bag, he put himself in jeopardy. Quick-thinking shortstop Derek Jeter took the throw from Jorge Posada and held the tag on Damon, who was called out following some discussion between the umpires and both managers. Jeter had also tagged out Luis Ugeto of the Seattle Mariners on a similar play in 2002.

CALL On a walk, the ball remains in play. If other runners are forced to advance, then they are allowed to walk to the next base. Any step beyond that base, however, and they are liable to be put out if tagged.

Answer 15: He is out.

16. JUST PASSING THROUGH

With runners on first and second and no one out, the batter hits the ball over the fence in left field. The runner from second base takes a few steps and watches the ball, thinking that it might be caught. In the meantime, the runner from first base puts his head down and runs past his teammate.

Question 16: Is either runner called out on this play? Does it still count as a home run?

GAME Late in the 1998 season, Kevin Young of the Cincinnati Reds hit an apparent three-run home run off of Pete Harnisch of the Pittsburgh Pirates. But when Jose Guillen ran past teammate Adrian Brown between second and third, he was called out for passing a leading runner. The home run stood, but only two runs counted.

In recent years, a number of runners have made this basic blunder and belong in a special hall of shame: Brady Anderson, Billy Ashley, Tony Fernandez, Cecil Fielder, Tom Lampkin, Miguel Ojeda, Terry Pendleton, Roberto Petagine, Alex Rodriguez, Ruben Sierra, Michael Tucker, Devon White, Lou Whittaker, and Eric Young.

A special mention goes to Terry Pendleton of the Atlanta Braves, who passed Deion Sanders during the 1992 World Series against the Toronto Blue Jays and almost caused a triple play. David Justice had hit a long fly ball to Devon White for the first out. Running from first base, Pendleton passed Sanders between second and third for the second out. And then Sanders was almost tagged out on appeal as he ran back to second.

CALL In most of the cases where a runner is called out for passing his teammate, there is some confusion over whether a fly ball will be caught. One runner is retreating to his base for safety, while a following runner steams ahead and passes him. It is always the following runner who is out in these situations.

Answer 16: The runner from first is out. It counts as a two-run home run.

17. SNEAKING AROUND

With two outs and runners on first and second, the batter hits a ground ball to the right side of the infield. The second baseman fields the ball and throws to the pitcher, who is running to cover first base while the first baseman is out of position. The pitcher catches the throw and beats the batter to first, but the umpire rules the runner safe because the pitcher failed to step on the bag. The pitcher, however, believes that his foot caught the edge of the base, and he argues with the first-base umpire. In the meantime, the other runners continue around the basepaths and cross home plate.

Question 17: During an argument with the umpire, can runners advance?

GAME Pitcher David Cone, playing for the New York Mets in 1990, was sure that he had stepped on first base to record the third out of a half-inning against the host Atlanta Braves. While he was pleading his case to umpire Charlie Williams, Atlanta runners Dale Murphy and Ernie Whitt took the opportunity to sneak around the basepaths. By the time Cone realized what was happening, both runners had scored. The Braves held on to win, 7–4.

CALL Many players assume that time is out automatically when they argue an umpire's decision. Time is never out automatically, except in special cases like foul balls or a hit batsman. Unless there is a play such as a balk or interference play where a timeout should be called, a player or manager needs to request a halt in the action. Then, umpires must decide whether a play is over. If the play is over, they can call a timeout or not, at their discretion. Once time is out, play does not restart until the pitcher steps on the rubber with the ball.

Answer 17: If time is not called, runners can advance at their own risk.

18. COUNTING TO THREE

The bases are loaded with one out when the batter hits a routine fly ball. The left fielder catches it and, thinking there are now three outs, he hands the ball to a young fan. When he sees the runners tagging up, he grabs the ball back from the startled spectator and throws to home plate, but by then two runs have scored.

Question 18: Could all three runners have scored if the fan kept the ball for himself?

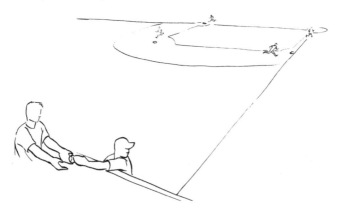

GAME In 2000, Benny Agbayani of the New York Mets joined a long tradition of ball players who have had trouble counting to three. Met pitcher Mike Hampton was trying to protect a 1–0 lead in the fourth inning against the visiting San Francisco Giants, when Agbayani gave the ball to a kid named Jake Burns. On Bobby Estalella's fly ball, San Francisco runners Jeff Kent and Ellis Burks both scored to take the lead and J.T. Snow went from first to third. Hampton then struck out pitcher Shawn Estes, stranding Snow at third base. Fortunately for Agbayani, the Mets came back to win, 3–2.

Before Agbayani's miscue, Larry Walker of the Montreal Expos was the Major Leaguer best known for handing a live ball to a fan. In 1994, Walker snagged a foul pop by Mike Piazza of the host Los Angeles Dodgers and handed it to a kid named Sebastian Nappier. By the time he realized his error and grabbed the ball back, Dodger runner Jose Offerman had gone from first to third. This did not make a significant difference to the game, which ended Dodgers 7, Expos 1.

In 2003, outfielder Trot Nixon of the Boston Red Sox became part of this trio of lameness when he also thought he had caught the third out of a half-inning and tossed the ball into the stands with two Anaheim Angels runners on base. This happened in the top of the ninth inning of a 3–2 game. On the play, Bengie Molina scored from second base to make the score 4–2, and Jeff DaVanon moved from first to third. Two more Angels soon scored, and the game finished 6–2.

CALL In these cases, handing the ball to a spectator is ruled exactly the same way as any overthrow. All runners are awarded two bases from the time of the throw (or hand-off). The ball is immediately dead.

Answer 18: No.

19. DESIGNATED MADNESS

During the late innings of an American League contest, the home team's manager sends the designated hitter in to play in the outfield. To make room for him, an outfielder leaves the game.

Question 19: Once the designated hitter comes in to play defense, can another player become the designated hitter or does the pitcher have to bat? Whatever you think the answer is, will the new designated hitter or pitcher then bat in place of the original designated hitter or in place of the player who has left the game?

GAME Manager Kevin Kennedy was never very clear about who should be pitching and who should be batting. In 1993, when he was with the Texas Rangers, he sent slugger Jose Canseco in to pitch, with disastrous consequences (see Question 54, on page 132). In 1996, after both he and Canseco had moved to the Boston Red Sox, he moved Canseco from the DH spot into left field. As a result, pitcher Roger Clemens had a rare American League at-bat.

This strange series of events happened in the eighth inning of a game in which the Red Sox had a commanding lead over the Seattle Mariners. You have to wonder—if it was a commanding lead, then why was it necessary to put Canseco into left field for defensive purposes? Was it worth risking injury to the great Roger Clemens, or was this merely a publicity stunt?

The "Rocket" had the last laugh that day, when he connected with a 0–2 pitch from Norm Charlton for a base hit. Clemens went on to pitch a scoreless ninth inning to preserve an 11–4 complete game victory.

CALL The designated hitter rule was introduced into the American League in 1973 for the simple and obvious reason that in the modern game, pitchers (despite Clemens's perfect batting record in 1996) are generally lousy hitters. The rule therefore allows for the offense to designate a hitter to bat in place of the pitcher. The DH cannot bat for any other defensive player.

Things can get a little confusing when substitutions are made. A pinch hitter can substitute for a DH and become the new DH. But if a DH comes in to play defense, then effectively the DH is lost. The pitcher would then take the place in the batting order of the player who leaves the game. This tactic is rarely used, but sometimes it does make sense, for example in an extra-inning game, when there are a lot of pinch hitters, by which point the pitchers tend not to stay in the game very long anyway and so may not come up to bat, and a manager may need to use the DH's particular defensive skills (especially if he is a catcher).

Answer 19: The pitcher has to bat and will take the place in the batting order of the player who has left the game.

The Appeal of the Game

A good understanding of the appeal play can be the difference between losing or winning a game. Let's see how familiar you are with the rules governing this simple yet often-misunderstood play.

20. HOWE TO APPEAL

With runners on first and third and one out, the batter hits a deep fly ball to center field. Just before the ball is caught, the runner on third takes off for home, scoring easily. The runner on first stays where he is. Seeing that the runner from third left early, the defense tries to organize an appeal play.

The pitcher takes the ball while standing on the rubber. He steps off, walks a few steps to third, and throws the ball to the third baseman. But the throw is wild and bounces into the stands. The plate umpire gives the pitcher a new ball, and he tries to appeal again, this time successfully making the throw to third.

Question 20: On the overthrow, is the runner from first base awarded any additional bases, even though he was not trying to advance on the play? Is this a proper appeal, and should the runner from third be called out, nullifying the run?

GAME This play changed the outcome of a game and almost signaled the end of a pitcher's career. The pitcher was former National League Rookie of the Year Steve Howe, appearing in relief for the New York Yankees against the Milwaukee Brewers in 1992. The visiting Brewers were mounting a comeback after trailing by six runs, and this play helped to turn the game around.

On the fly ball to Roberto Kelly in center field, Dante Bichette was the runner who left early from third. When Howe then threw the ball into the stands, runner Dave Nilsson was awarded two bases, moving him from first to third. On the second attempt at an appeal, umpire Rich

Garcia ruled that it was an improper appeal, meaning that Bichette's run counted despite the fact that he had clearly left his base before the catch.

This made the score Yankees 9, Brewers 7, with only one out and a runner on third. Had Howe successfully made his first throw to third baseman Charlie Hayes—or if he had simply walked over to third base with the ball—Bichette would have been called out on appeal for leaving the base early, and the score would have been 9–6, with two outs and a runner on first. Eventually, the Brewers completed their comeback and won the game in 14 innings, 10–9. Bichette's run made the difference by helping to force the game into extra innings.

Two weeks after this game, Howe, who had already been suspended from baseball six times for drug-related offenses, admitted that again he had tried to buy cocaine. A month after the incident, he was banned permanently from baseball. That November, an arbitrator ruled that Howe's cocaine abuse stemmed from his attention deficit disorder and reinstated him. Howe went on to play for the Yankees for four more years, but was released in June, 1996, just missing the start of the Yankees' run of World Series victories. Within days of his release from the team, Howe was arrested at the airport because he had a loaded gun in his suitcase. Tragically, Howe's troubled life came to a premature end in a car accident.

CALL Steve Howe was an exceptionally talented player with a very serious problem. Some say that he had the potential to be one of the great relief pitchers in baseball.

This is a sad story with clear lessons about the dangers of illegal drugs. In this case, the pitcher's failure to make an unhurried throw to third base from about 50 feet away may have revealed underlying difficulties in his personal life, or perhaps it was just one of those unlucky plays. What the incident certainly shows is that there are widespread misconceptions about what is required to make a successful appeal, and the Yankees made the play harder than it needed to be.

In this play, there were two unusual rules, starting with the overthrow. When a player throws the ball out of play, all base runners are awarded two additional bases from their position at the time of the throw. The main exception to this is when an infielder throws the ball out of play just after a batter makes contact, in which case the two-base award is measured from the time of the pitch.

In the Steve Howe example, there was no pitch—no chance for the batter to put the ball in play—and the two bases were awarded from the time Howe threw the ball over Hayes's head. Nilsson was able to advance all the way to third, even though he was standing on first base at the time of the play. There is another exception to the two-base rule (see Question 5, on page 10).

The other unusual rule in our example is the improper appeal. The idea behind an appeal play is that the defense must earn every out. When a runner leaves his base early, the umpire will act as if nothing has happened unless the defense attempts to make a play.

After making the catch, Roberto Kelly could have thrown the ball directly to Charlie Hayes for the appeal at third. Instead, the Yankees unnecessarily called for a timeout and then had to begin live play again by giving the ball to the pitcher, who then had to stand on the rubber to end the timeout. Once Howe had the ball and had stepped off the mound, he could have walked to third base. Instead, he chose to throw the ball.

The defense only gets one chance to appeal a particular play. If the team commits an error, as Steve Howe did, the out is no longer deserved, and play proceeds as if the infraction never occurred. This is why on Howe's second attempt to appeal third, the umpire signaled neither out nor safe—he no longer recognized the appeal. It was as if Dante Bichette had left after the catch, and his run counted.

Answer 20: The runner from first is awarded two bases. It is an improper appeal, and the run counts.

DEFINITION: APPEAL PLAY

An appeal play is when the defense claims that the offense violated the rules. Some appeal plays can be made verbally, while others require special actions like stepping on a base while in possession of the ball. If the defense does not appeal or appeals incorrectly, then play proceeds as if no violation took place.

21. THE GHOST RUN

Runners are on first and third with one out. The batter attempts to bunt but pops up to the pitcher. Both runners are trying to advance and are well off their bases when the ball is caught. The pitcher then throws to the first baseman to record the third out. Pleased that the double-play ends the half-inning, the defense leaves the field. But in the meantime, the runner from third, who never retouched his base after the out, had crossed home plate before the out at first.

Question 21: Does the run count?

GAME The Yankees were playing the Brewers again at Yankee Stadium, only this time the roles were reversed. In July, 1989, the Yankees were batting, trying to add to their 4–1 lead. Batter Wayne Tolleson offered the bunt, with runners Bob Geren (from first) and Mike Pagliarulo (from third) moving on the pitch. Pitcher Jay Aldrich made the catch just as the ball was about to hit the ground and then threw to first baseman Greg Brock for the third out. This third out was an appeal play because Geren had left early. Pagliarulo had also left early, but because no one appealed third base, the play proceeded as if he had tagged up.

Once the Brewers left the field, plate umpire Larry Barnett ruled that Pagliarulo's run counted. The play was so unusual that the official scorer didn't believe it. For the rest of the game, the scoreboard showed the score as 4–1, when in fact it was 5–1. This had no bearing on the outcome of the game except that relief pitcher Lee Guetterman did not earn a save, because Pagliarulo's run meant that the Yankees' lead was greater than three runs. After the game, Yankee manager Dallas Green said he had never seen anything like it before.

These so-called "phantom runs" are very rare. The first recorded instance of one was in 1957 in the old Pacific Coast League. At the time, the PCL was "open classification," which meant that it acted as a sort of third Major League. In a similar situation, umpire Al Somers declared that a run had scored even though the runner from third had failed to tag up. Manager Joe "Flash" Gordon of the San

Francisco Seals protested the game. Somers had a reputation as one of the game's most knowledgeable umpires, and the rule book was soon changed to account for his interpretation of the play. "They thought I was crazy," Somers said. "I'll tell you one thing—I didn't think I would be able to get out of the stadium that night."

During the same season, there were two other "phantom runs," one in the International League in a game between the Buffalo Bisons and Toronto Maple Leafs, and one in the American League that involved the Boston Red Sox and Cleveland Indians. With Boston runners on first and second with one out, Cleveland shortstop Chico Carrasquel made a diving catch in short left field. By the time he completed a double play with a throw to first base, runner Gene Mauch had scored all the way from second. Umpire Hank Soar later awarded the run, which made the score Boston 11, Cleveland 0.

Cal Hubbard, the American League umpire supervisor, later explained, "If they know the rules, they'll know what to do. If not, it's their tough luck." This was a little disingenuous because the rule book was not changed to account for this situation until the following year. But today's players have no excuse!

CALL The most confusing aspect to the "phantom run" stems from the common misconception that no run can score on a play where the third out is made. It is true that in many cases no run can score on a play that ends a half-inning. There are two basic types of half-inning-ending plays: (1) plays where the batter makes the third out before reaching first base and (2) plays where the batter either reaches first base or, if he fails to reach first base, plays where he does not make the third out himself. On the first type of play, no run can score no matter what else happens. The second type of play is a timing play, and runs can score if they occur before the third out. The one exception to this simple rule is a force play. When the third out is a force out, then no run can score because a force out is considered to be, in effect, the same as the batter not reaching first base.

In the first example above, batter Wayne Tolleson made the second out, not the third out. Once the batter was out, the force situation was removed, and Bob Geren retained his right to first base. At this point, it became a timing play. The question was whether the third out would be recorded before the run scored.

Once the Brewers made the third out, they were in a difficult situation. The rule book states that a half-inning has only three outs. As it happened, Milwaukee ignored the runner from third. But what if they wanted to appeal third base after the third out? Would Pagliarulo's run still count?

The rule book has an answer for this, and it is called an apparent "fourth out." If the Brewers had been more aware of the situation, then after the play they could have taken the ball to third base, recording an out on Pagliarulo on appeal, which would replace the out on Geren in the official scoring. It would look like the Brewers made four outs in the inning, when in reality they would still have just made three, since Geren's out would be withdrawn. It would not count as a triple-play. This is the fairest way to protect the defense from having a run scored against them that is not deserved. But they must pay attention and make the appeal. Officially, the defense can make an apparent "fourth out" at any time until the pitcher and all the infielders have left fair territory on their way back to the dugout.

This is all theory. In practice, the play is very rare. I am not aware of an apparent "fourth out" ever actually being recorded in the Major Leagues. But stay tuned, and you may just see one!

Answer 21: Yes.

DEFINITION: FORCE OUT

A force out can occur when a runner loses his right to his base because the batter becomes a runner (usually after hitting the ball). Runners are forced when there is no open base between them and the batter. Force outs can be recorded by tagging the runner or tagging the base to which he is advancing.

---

22. TOUCHING THEM ALL

A runner leads off first base with one out when the batter hits a line drive. The third baseman catches the ball and then tries for a double play by throwing to first, where the runner has not tagged up and is off the base. But the throw is wild and goes out of play. The umpires call time and award the runner two bases on the overthrow.

Question 22: When the ball is dead on an overthrow, can the runner still return to his base to tag up? Does he need to tag up or does the overthrow nullify the defense's chance to appeal? What are the two bases awarded to him—first and second, or second and third?

GAME It is amazing how many Major League baseball players do not understand that they must touch all of the bases in order. Perhaps Melvin Mora of the Baltimore Orioles was still rusty from the off-season when he forgot this basic baseball principle on opening day in 2001.

Trailing the visiting Boston Red Sox, 1–0, the Orioles were rallying in the fifth inning. With Mora leading off first base, Brook Fordyce lined out to third baseman Shea Hillenbrand, who threw the ball into the crowd in an attempt for a double play. The umpires awarded Mora third base, which he took without bothering to go to second. When Red Sox ace Pedro Martinez put the ball back in play, he made a successful appeal at second, ending the threat and the half-inning.

The Orioles scored in the next inning, thanks to an RBI single by Mike Bordick, and then went on to win in 11 innings, 2–1. It's too bad that Bordick had not paid better attention to his teammate's baserunning miscue, because he made a similar mistake two years later.

In 2003, playing for the Toronto Blue Jays, Bordick found himself in Mora's position in a game against the host Texas Rangers. Bordick was running from first base when Vernon Wells hit a line drive. The ball deflected off Ranger pitcher Colby Lewis and straight into the glove of third baseman Hank Blalock for an out. By this point, Bordick was rounding second. Blalock then fired the ball into the crowd behind first base. On the overthrow, Bordick continued on to third base without retagging first.

After Texas manager Buck Showalter checked that Lewis was not injured, Lewis put the ball in play and retired Bordick, on appeal, at second base, ending the half inning. The Rangers went on to win, 5–4.

CALL Even when a runner is awarded bases on an overthrow, he must still tag up and touch all the bases in order, or else he puts himself at risk of being called out on appeal. Both Mora and Bordick needed to retouch first base after the ball had gone out of play, and then proceed to second before finally advancing to third. Neither of them did this, but they each took different routes to third base.

Mora failed to touch both first and second base and simply proceeded to third on the overthrow by cutting across the diamond. He could have been called out on appeal at either base (or by being tagged).

Bordick's miscue is a little more complicated. Because he had already passed second base, he would have had to retouch second, then retouch first, then step on second base a third time before proceeding to third base. According to the rules, however, when the ball is dead (as in the overthrow), a runner cannot go back and retouch a base after he has already reached the next base. Bordick's only chance of retouching first would be if he had already returned to second base by the time the ball went out of play.

In Bordick's case, the Rangers really should have made the appeal at first base. Instead, they appealed at second, which Bordick had actually touched after he failed to tag up at first base. It seems that the umpires reasoned that Bordick's failure to retouch second base (as would have been required had he gone back to retouch first base) was enough to warrant calling him out at that base as well. The rule book does not actually discuss this situation. But common sense tells us that the Rangers made a good appeal and that Bordick had run the bases incorrectly, so he deserved to be called out.

These overthrows do not nullify the defense's ability to appeal, despite the fact that teams only have one chance to appeal a particular play, because in a sense the runners committed an additional violation when they failed to retouch a base during the dead ball.

Answer 22: On a dead ball, a runner can return to tag up, as long as he has not already advanced to the next base. Despite being awarded additional bases and despite the overthrow, he does need to tag up or he is at risk of being called out on appeal. On an overthrow, he is awarded two bases from his last legally acquired base, which in this case means he gets second and third.

Order of the day

In cases of batting out of order, at least one of the two man-agers is guilty of the kind of mistake that can cost his team the game. It is tough to know what is more surprising—that this happens as often as it does or that so few managers have figured out how to use the rule to their advantage. Either way, it has led to some funny situations. Here are two.

23. FROM CIRCLE TO BOX

Runners are on second and third with one out when the bat-ter hits a sacrifice fly to score the man from third base. The problem is that this batter was not due up yet. According to the lineup, he should have been in the on-deck circle rather than the batter's box. Following this, the batter whose turn had just been skipped comes in to hit.

Question 23: Is the play allowed to stand, despite the batting out of order? The call is on page 60.

GAME Baltimore Orioles batter Jay Gibbons was in the fourth slot in the batting order and Tony Batista was in the fifth slot during a game against the visiting New York Yankees in 2003. But in the first inning, Batista jumped in

front of Gibbons and got an RBI in this batting out-of-turn situation. Yankee manager Joe Torre did not notice and did not appeal, so the umpires let play proceed without reference to the miscue. Had Torre appealed, Gibbons would have been called out, the runners would have returned to second and third, and Batista would have been due up again.

The moment the next pitch came in to Gibbons, however, Batista's at-bat became legal. This meant that the run stood and the next proper batter due up was the person in the sixth slot in the lineup, Brook Fordyce. Gibbons, also batting out of turn, was retired to end the inning. But, by the time the Orioles batted again, Gibbons's at-bat had become legal, so the next batter should have been the person who followed him in the order—Tony Batista! Instead, Fordyce batted and made an out. For the rest of the game, Baltimore went back to the correct batting order.

Baltimore's first-inning run made a big difference in this crazy game, which featured a blown save in the ninth inning by the Yankees' Mariano Rivera, a 12th-inning home run by teammate Jason Giambi, and one of the weirdest plays ever to end a game.

In the bottom of the 12th, with the Yankees now leading 5–4, the Orioles had Jack Cust on first base with two outs when Larry Bigbie hit the ball deep to right field. Cust ran all the way past third base and got caught in a rundown. The Yankees misplayed the situation, however, and let Cust sneak past catcher Jorge Posada with no one defending home plate. With a mere 25 feet to go to score the tying run and no one standing in his way, Cust fell down, and was tagged out by Aaron Boone.

In this play, Cust's slip-up lost the game for the Orioles and drew attention away from the embarrassing fact that Torre's failure to appeal was the reason the game was in extra innings in the first place. This was a rare mistake by Torre, who had a history of understanding batting-out-of-order situations. In a game in 1996, Torre's appeal nullified a single by Matt Mieske of the Milwaukee Brewers, who had batted in place of Jose Valentin. Valentin was called out, bringing up Mieske again, who hit a pop fly. Despite the setback, the Brewers won that day, 4–1.

24. INVISIBLE DOUBLE SWITCH

The home team's manager replaces his shortstop and pitcher in the top of the seventh, but he does not indicate to the umpire where these players will bat in the batting order. The umpire assumes that they will each bat in the place of the person whose defensive position they are replacing. In the bottom of the seventh, with the pitcher due up, the short-stop comes in and hits a double. The visiting manager appeals for batting out of order.

Question 24: Does the double still count? Is either the short-stop or the pitcher called out? The call is on page 60.

GAME Early in 2004, Cubs manager Dusty Baker was guilty of not informing the umpires of this "double-switch," where an additional lineup change is made while replacing the pitcher in order to move the pitcher's place further down in the batting order. With Cincinnati Reds manager Dave Miley already ejected from the game after he had argued a called strike, substitute manager Jerry Narron alerted the umpires to the out-of-order situation.

Ramon Martinez was the unlucky shortstop whose double was erased from the books after the appeal. Pitcher Kent Mercker was called out for failing to bat in the correct spot. Dusty Baker did not take this well. He argued with the umpires, threw his hat twice, threw his copy of the lineup card, kicked a bat, and got ejected from the game.

Despite having the double nullified, the Cubs won in dramatic fashion in the bottom of the ninth when Sammy Sosa and Moises Alou hit home runs on consecutive pitches to make the score Cubs 11, Reds 10.

This was not Baker's first experience of batting out of order. In 1980, as a player, he batted in place of Los Angeles Dodger teammate Ron Cey, who was actually due to bat. After Baker grounded out, Cey was called out following an appeal by Philadelphia Phillies manager Dallas Green, and Baker's at-bat was nullified. This brought up the batter who followed Cey in the order—Dusty Baker. Given a second chance, Baker hit a three-run home run which proved decisive in a 12–10 victory.

CALL Batting out of turn can seem confusing to managers, players, and fans. But the rule is actually very simple if you remember these easy guidelines:

Batting out of order is an appeal play, so the game continues as normal until the defense notifies the umpires of the infraction.

If the appeal occurs after the improper batter completes an at-bat, the play is nullified (although stolen bases, balks, etc., still count), the proper batter is called out, and the next batter is the one that follows the proper batter in the order.

If the appeal comes before the at-bat is over, then there is no out recorded and the proper batter comes in to bat, inheriting the ball/strike count that the improper batter had.

In the absence of an appeal after an improper batter completes an at-bat, if a pitch is then thrown to the next batter or if there is some other play, then the improper batter becomes, retroactively, the proper batter. This is the tricky part of the rule, but it makes sense if you remember that without an appeal, the game proceeds as if there had been no infraction. It explains why, in the Yankees–Orioles game, Tony Batista was not the only person who batted out of order. Gibbons was also out of order when he followed Batista, and Fordyce was out of order when he followed Gibbons.

In theory, it is possible that through some arcane process of players batting out of order that the next proper batter would already be on base. In this unlikely case, the player's spot in the order can be skipped.

Here are the answers:

23. The play stands because there was no appeal.

24. The double is nullified and the pitcher is called out.

Right of Way

Inevitably, base runners and defensive players will cross paths on the baseball diamond. Players and fans have also been known to clash. In such cases, it's important to know who has the right to be somewhere and who is in the wrong.

25. STAY IN LANE

The batter hits a "squibber"—a weak ground ball that is fielded by the catcher. On the way to first base, the batter runs with one foot on the infield side of the 45-foot running lane. The catcher's throw is high, and the batter makes it to first base safely.

Question 25: Is the batter out for interference?

GAME   The New York Yankees were visiting the Toronto Blue Jays in 2004 when this play occurred. After fielding a weak ground ball by Blue Jay Alex Rios, Yankee catcher

Jorge Posada threw high to first base. Even though the throw did not hit the runner, Rios caused Posada to alter the trajectory of the attempted put-out when he ran outside of his running lane. Rios was called out for interference in a game that New York won, 7–4, after having trailed 4–0.

Perhaps the most famous play involving these mysterious lines in second half of the route to first base occurred in the second game of the 1998 American League Championship Series between the Yankees and the Cleveland Indians. Cleveland's Travis Fryman bunted in the 12th inning with the score tied, 1–1. New York first baseman Tino Martinez threw to Chuck Knoblauch, covering the bag, but the ball hit Fryman in the back as he was running outside of the lane, on the infield grass.

In this case, the umpires did not call interference, even though replays showed that Fryman ran the entire 45 feet outside of the running lane. This was a rare umpiring gaffe, but one that was not quite so destructive as the one Knoblauch made on the play. Instead of running after the ball, Knoblauch remained at first base to argue the umpire's decision. In the meantime, Enrique Wilson scored the go-ahead run and Fryman made it to second base. Later, Knoblauch might have discussed this play with teammate David Cone, who had some experience arguing with umpires while his opponents rounded the bases. The Indians soon won the game, 4–1, but lost the series, 4–2.

CALL Years ago, before I became an umpire, while watching a minor league game in Maine, I asked no one in particular, *what is the meaning of that lane on the second half of the baseline between home and first?* A local fan turned around and said sarcastically that I must be new to baseball. In fact, I had watched the game for years, but I never understood the rules that apply to the lane until I went to umpire school.

The lane, which is on the foul-territory side of the first-base line, makes it possible for the batter to run to first base without risking interference. On a bunt or short ground ball, the fielder will have to throw the ball around the runner. If the runner has one or both of his feet outside of the three-foot-wide lane, then he should be called out for interference if his body gets in the way of the throw. If he is entirely within the lane and the throw hits him, then the ball remains in play.

The ball must actually be thrown for there to be interference, but it does not actually have to hit the runner. Many times, I have seen a pitcher or catcher hold back from throwing to first base when the runner is clearly outside of the running lane. All they would need to do is throw the ball, and the runner would be called out. The umpire does not need to judge whether the runner would have been out were it not for the interference. If there is interference, there will be an out. It really does pay for players to know the rules!

Answer 25: He is out for interference.

DEFINITION: INTERFERENCE PART 1 (OFFENSIVE)

It is offensive interference when a member of the batting team illegally prevents a fielder from making a play.

---

26. ALTER COURSE

Leading off an inning, a batter hits the ball to center field and tries to stretch his hit into a double. While rounding first, however, he has to alter course slightly in order to avoid colliding with the first baseman, who is watching the ball. Sliding into second, he is tagged out on a close play.

Question 26: Is this considered interference, obstruction, or neither? If one of the two, what is the penalty?

GAME In 2000, the Yankees and Mets faced off at Shea Stadium in the first game of a rare day-night doubleheader in which both teams hosted a game. This unusual situation, which saw an estimated 30,000 fans use the subway to go from one stadium to the other, came about following a rain-out earlier in the season. The nightcap at Yankee Stadium would be remembered for Yankee pitcher Roger Clemens's beaning of Met catcher Mike Piazza in the head. But in the first game, controversy surrounded the very first pitch.

Yankee Chuck Knoblauch hit a single up the middle and tried to make it a double, but center fielder Jay Payton threw him out at second base. Umpire Robb Cook, however, ruled Knoblauch safe and cited Met first baseman Todd Zeile with obstruction for standing in the basepath. According to Cook, Knoblauch would have made it to second safely if he did not have to run around Zeile, so he awarded Knoblauch second base. Host manager Bobby Valentine was so upset that he tried to show the umpires the path Knoblauch took, and he was quickly ejected for inciting the crowd.

Knoblauch soon scored, and the Yankees led, 2–0, after the first inning. To find out how the game ended, read the next question.

CALL In this play, common sense tells us that runners have the right to the basepaths when fielders are not involved in a play. Knoblauch should not have had to move even one step in order to avoid Zeile. He was delayed by the fraction of a second that may have cost him reaching second base safely, and the umpires disallowed the putout and awarded him second base.

The most confusing aspect to this play is the terminology, which is often misunderstood by players, managers, broadcasters, and newspaper reporters. When the defense gets in the way of a runner, it is called *obstruction*. When the offense gets in the way of a fielder, it is called *interference*. Confusingly, when the catcher gets in the way of a batter, it is also called interference, rather than obstruction.

Answer 26: Obstruction. The runner is awarded second base.

DEFINITION: OBSTRUCTION

Obstruction is when a member of defensive team, while not holding the ball or fielding the ball, slows the advance of a runner.

---

27. CRASH

With a runner on first base and two outs, the batter hits a routine ground ball to the second baseman. But the second baseman fields the ball directly in the basepath between first and second, and the runner from first makes contact with him.

Question 27: Who had the right of way in this instance, and who is guilty of obstruction or interference? What is the penalty?

GAME In the fourth inning of the same Yankees–Mets game as in the previous question, Todd Zeile was standing on first when Jay Payton hit a ground ball to Yankee second baseman Chuck Knoblauch. (Remember that in the first inning, Knoblauch had hit a ball to Payton and was obstructed by Zeile!) Perhaps Zeile was trying to take revenge on Knoblauch by running into him on the basepath. But this time, the umpires ruled interference and called Zeile automatically out.

Within the space of a few innings, Zeile had committed both obstruction and interference. The Yankees went on to win both games that day by identical scores of 4–2.

At the end of the 2000 season, the Yankees and Mets squared off again in the World Series. The result was the same, with the Bronx Bombers defeating their Queens rivals.

CALL Obstruction and interference are easy to understand if you remember the following principles: When the defense is fielding a batted ball, the runners must get out of the way or risk being called out for interference; when the defense is not fielding the ball, the runners have full rights to the basepaths or they may become victims of obstruction.

These terms apply only to runners and fielders. When a batter is trying to hit (see Question 46), his action has the right of way over the catcher, who may be guilty of catcher's interference if his act of catching the pitch gets in the way of the swing. There are also rules that cover umpire's interference, in which the umpire hinders the defense (like when a batted ball hits an umpire or when the umpire blocks the catcher's attempted putout of a runner stealing a base).

Answer 27: The fielder has the right to field the ball. The runner is guilty of interference and is automatically out. If there had been fewer than two outs, and if the umpires had judged that the runner interfered intentionally, then two outs would have been charged.

28. GOING BACK

Now that you have mastered the basics of obstruction and interference from the previous two questions, here's a twist on the scenario:

Caught in a rundown between third and home, a base runner is chased back to third by the catcher. The catcher throws to the shortstop, covering the bag, but in the meantime, the runner collides with the third baseman, who is standing in his way.

Question 28: Is this interference or obstruction, and what is the penalty?

GAME Proving the maxim that when it rains, it pours, there were no fewer than three highly unusual possible obstruction plays during a 2003 playoff game between the Oakland A's and Boston Red Sox. This was one of the closest-fought playoff series in recent memory. Oakland had won the first game, 5–4, in 12 innings, after tying the score in the bottom of the ninth. The A's then won the second game, 5–1, and were on the verge of winning the best-of-five series when it moved to Boston for the third game.

With the score 0–0 in the bottom of the second inning of Game 3, two Oakland errors put Red Sox runners on first and third with one out. Then Damian Jackson hit a grounder to third baseman Eric Chavez, trapping teammate Jason Varitek in a rundown between third and home. A's catcher Ramon Hernandez chased Varitek almost all the way back to third, when Varitek ran into Chavez.

The umpires called obstruction on Chavez and awarded Varitek home base. This proved to be the Red Sox's only run until the 11th inning. In the meantime, there were two other controversial possible obstruction plays, both of which also went in the Red Sox's favor.

In the top of the sixth inning, the A's were threatening to score, with runners on first and third and one out. Miguel Tejada hit a ground ball to pitcher Derek Lowe, who tried to nab Oakland runner Eric Byrnes at home plate. Varitek, the Boston catcher, lunged for Lowe's poor throw, which flew past him and went all the way to the backstop. But in doing so, his body blocked the progress of Byrnes, who injured his ankle and started to limp back to the dugout under the mis-apprehension that he had touched the plate. In the collision, Byrnes missed the plate, and Varitek gathered the ball and tagged him out.

Because Varitek blocked Byrnes in the process of field-ing the throw, it was not considered to be obstruction. Now there were two outs, and an intentional walk loaded the bases. The next batter was Hernandez, the Oakland catcher, who hit a ground ball that found its way past the glove of Red Sox shortstop Nomar Garciaparra for an error. Then lightning struck a third time.

Erubiel Durazo scored as Manny Ramirez got to the ball and fired it home. While rounding third base, Oakland run-ner Tejada was obstructed by Boston's Bill Mueller. Upon hearing the obstruction call, Tejada all but stopped running and was tagged out by Varitek. The umpires ruled that Tejada would not have scored on the play, and so the out stood.

The score remained at 1–1 until the bottom of the 11th inning when pinch hitter Trot Nixon hit a game-end-ing two-run home run. The Red Sox went on to take the series with a dramatic come-from-behind 5–4 win in Game 4 and a 4–3 victory in the decisive fifth game. Their luck finally ran out, however, in the 11th inning of the seventh and final game of the American League Championship Series against the New York Yankees.

CALL The penalty for obstruction depends on the circum-stances surrounding it. If it occurs when a play is not being made on a player, as in the Chuck Knoblauch example in Question 26, then the award is the base that the runner would have gotten had the obstruction not taken place. However, when a play is being made on a player, the penalty for the obstruction must be at least one additional base. When a play is not being made on a runner, it is a delayed dead ball. When a play is being made on a runner, the ball is dead immediately.

At first glance, this rule may seem unfair. In our example, Jason Varitek was running back to third base when he was obstructed, and yet he was awarded home and scored a run— a decisive run, as it happened. But the penalty is logical when you consider that awarding him third base would have been no penalty at all, since he had already obtained third base safely. When a runner is returning to a base, the defense would have almost nothing to lose by attempting to obstruct him, if the penalty did not involve the award of an additional base. The lesson here is that there is a strong disincentive to getting in the way of runners.

The other controversial calls in the A's–Red Sox playoff game illustrate further aspects of the obstruction rule. During the plateside collision between Varitek and Byrnes, both players had equal rights to be where they were— Varitek was fielding a thrown ball (not a batted ball, or else he would have had the right of way) and Byrnes was running the basepath—and so no obstruction or interference was called.

On the obstruction against Tejada, he was awarded third base (which he had not yet reached when Mueller got in his way). When he then slowed down, he effectively prevented the umpires from granting him home. Had he run his fastest and been thrown out by a whisker, then the umpires would probably have awarded the run. But when he stopped running, he removed his best argument that he could have made it home had the obstruction not taken place.

Answer 28: Obstruction. He is awarded home base.

29. SLIDING INTO NOWHERE

With runners on first and third and one out, the batter hits a ground ball for a possible double play. After the shortstop touches second base holding the ball, he steps away from the bag in order to make a clear throw to first. But the runner from first tries to break up the double play by sliding underneath the shortstop, even though this means his slide takes him away from the base. In the end, the runner's slide has no effect on the throw to first, which was too late to complete the double play.

Question 29: Is this interference on the part of the runner from first base, even though the batter would have made it to first base anyway?

GAME The score was knotted 2–2, when the Chicago Cubs were attempting a rally against the host Philadelphia Phillies in 2003. With Jose Hernandez on third and Cub pitcher Carlos Zambrano standing on first, Mark Grudzielanek hit into this potential double play to end the half-inning. Instead of sliding toward second base, Zambrano slid toward Phillies shortstop Jimmy Rollins, whose throw would not have beaten Grudzielanek to first.

This was ruled interference, and Grudzielanek was also called out, nullifying Hernandez's potential run home from third. This double play ended the threat and left the score tied at 2–2. Philadelphia went on to score 10 more times and won, 12–2.

CALL On an interference play like this, the umpires do not have to judge whether the interference was actually effective in preventing an out from being recorded. Other than obvious plays, such a call would be impossible to judge in any case, especially when the difference between out and safe is often measured in tiny fractions of a second. The penalty for interference is an out, regardless of what *would* have happened. Zambrano interfered with Rollins's attempt to put out Grudzielanek, and so Grudzielanek was called out.

Answer 29: It is interference. The batter is also called out.

30. SLAP-HAPPY

A runner stands on first base with one out when the batter hits a ground ball up the first base line. The pitcher fields the ball and tries to tag the batter. But the batter slaps the ball out of the pitcher's glove. The ball rolls all the way to the outfield, allowing the runner from first to score and the batter to reach second base.

Question 30: Is this a legal play or is it interference?

GAME Many baseball fans will recognize this play from the epic 2004 American League Championship Series between the Boston Red Sox and New York Yankees. The Yankees had won the first three games of the series, but then lost the next two.

In Game 6, the Yankees were trailing when Derek Jeter singled home a run to make the score Boston 4, New York 2. Then Alex Rodriguez hit a ground ball toward first base. Pitcher Bronson Arroyo gathered it up and tried to apply a tag when the ball came loose.

Umpire Randy Marsh initially ruled Rodriguez safe, and it looked as though New York had made the score 4–3 with a runner in scoring position. But after Marsh conferred with the other umpires, who had a better view of the play, Rodriguez was called out for interference. The fan reaction was so violent that umpires had to clear the field, and there was a risk of the game being forfeited to the Red Sox. Order was restored, however, Jeter was sent back to first, and the game eventually ended as it was then, 4–2 to Boston. The Red Sox went on to win Game 7 and swept the World Series for their first championship since 1918.

CALL Common sense tells us that runners do not have the right to slap the ball out of the hands or gloves of the defense.

In these cases, the runner is out for interference, and no other runners can advance on the play. If the interference prevents a double-play, then two outs would be charged.

The key to judging interference is the intent of the runner. In this example, Rodriguez clearly tried to knock the ball loose. Slapping at the ball is not a natural part of running to first base.

Often there will be a collision and a dropped ball during a play at the plate. When a runner trying to score collides with a catcher making a play on him and the catcher drops the ball, then the umpire must decide whether the collision was caused by the runner going home or by the runner going specifically for the ball. In plays at the plate, the umpire must also judge whether the catcher, before he gets the ball, intentionally blocks the path of the runner or is in the process of fielding the throw home. If he is blocking the plate without the ball, then he is obstructing the runner.

Answer 30: Interference. The batter is out, and the runner returns to first.

31. BLIND SPOT

The home team has runners on first and third with one out in a game that is tied in extra innings. The batter hits a fly ball to left field, just about far enough to become a sacrifice fly that could score the winning run. The runner on third has trouble seeing the catch because the short-stop is blocking his view. After the catch, the runner takes a few steps toward home and then retreats to the safety of third base.

Question 31: Is this obstruction and should the runner be awarded home plate?

GAME Clever infielders sometimes try to gain an unfair advantage by preventing runners from getting a clear view of a catch. In 2004, the clever infielder was Jose Lopez of the Seattle Mariners. Tino Martinez of the Tampa Bay Devil Rays flied out to Raul Ibanez in left field. Runner Carl Crawford broke for home, but then returned to third base.

Umpire Paul Emmel called obstruction. Because Emmel felt that Crawford could have scored if he had had a better view of the catch, he awarded him home plate. This play ended the game, with the score Tampa Bay 2, Seattle 1.

CALL Obstruction is an act by the defense that impedes the progress of a runner. Normally, obstruction occurs when a fielder stands in the basepaths and blocks the route a runner is taking around the bases. But this play shows that obstruction can take other forms as well. The penalty is for the runners to be awarded the bases they would have reached if the obstruction had not occurred.

Answer 31: Yes, it was obstruction, and the runner should be awarded home plate.

Fans 3, fielders 0

Many fans like to bring their baseball gloves to a game with the hope of coming away with a treasured souvenir. Sometimes, however, fans become a little overexcited by the prospect of owning a real Major League baseball and interfere with live play. It is one thing to catch a foul ball or a home run. It is something else altogether to try to grab a ball that a fielder is trying to reach. While reaching for a live ball is not always interference, it is almost always inadvisable.

32. DEFLECTED

The home team is trailing by two runs in the bottom of the ninth with two outs and the bases loaded. The batter hits a fair ball into the left field corner, where a fan leans over and tries to grab it. He does not hold on, and the ball glances off of his hand and deflects back into fair territory.

Question 32: Is this interference and, if so, how many runs can score on the play? The call is on page 85.

GAME The Texas Rangers were trailing the visiting Chicago White Sox, 6–3, in the final frame of this nail-biter in 1991. With the help of an error, a walk, a hit batsman, and just one base hit, the Rangers had managed to claw back a run and load the bases. With two outs and the potential winning run on first, pinch hitter Monty Fariss came in to face Chicago reliever Bobby Thigpen. Rafael Palmiero was standing on third base, Reuben Sierra was on second, and Juan Gonzales was on first.

Fariss hit the ball hard into the corner, where it was touched by a fan. Third base umpire Joe Brinkman held his arms above his head and clasped his wrist to indicate fan interference. The three other umpires judged that if the fan had not interfered, then all three runners would have been able to score. This was the award they made, and the Rangers instantly won the game, 7–6. Many fans were left wondering what had happened because it is so unusual to see a runner—in this case Gonzales—awarded three bases during a dead ball situation.

33. STOLEN

In the eighth inning of a playoff game, trailing by one run, a batter for the home team hits a deep fly ball toward the right field fence. The right fielder arrives to make the catch, and just as the ball appears to reach the top of the wall, a fan swipes it for himself.

Question 33: Is this a home run or an automatic out? The call is on page 85.

GAME The Baltimore Orioles were visiting Yankee Stadium for the first game of the American League Championship Series in 1996. Neither team had won a World Series in more than a decade, and the level of excitement was high. Baltimore was ahead, 4–3, when New York's Derek Jeter hit a ball that looked as though it just might clear the short right field fence for a home run and draw the game even at 4–4.

Baltimore's Tony Tarasco thought he had a good chance to make a catch when 12-year-old Jeffrey Maier wrote himself into baseball history. Umpire Rich Garcia ruled it a home run. Garcia later admitted that from a different angle, replays showed that the ball had not yet cleared the fence and Maier had stolen the ball from Tarasco. Because this was a judgment call, Oriole manager Davey Johnson had no grounds for appeal. The Yankees went on to win the game, 5–4, in extra innings thanks to a home run by Bernie Williams. They also won the ALCS and the World Series.

34. CURSED

Also in the eighth inning of a playoff game, the visiting team is behind by three runs with one out and a man on second. The batter hits a foul pop close to the seats down the third base line. The left fielder, reaching over the fence, has a good chance at the catch, but the ball is deflected away by a fan in the front row.

Question 34: Is this a foul ball or an automatic out? The call is on page 85.

GAME With plays like this one, it's no wonder that baseball fans are among the most superstitious people in the world. In 2003, the Chicago Cubs seemed on the verge of their first World Series appearance since 1945 when disaster struck.

Cub left fielder Moises Alou looked like he might catch Luis Castillo's foul pop, which drifted about one foot into the stands. Cub fan Steve Bartman, oblivious to Alou's presence, unwittingly robbed his team of a crucial out when he made contact with the ball. Umpire Mike Everitt ruled no interference because the ball was no longer over the playing field when Bartman touched it.

At this point, Chicago collapsed. After the non-catch, Castillo walked. Then there was a wild pitch, followed by a base hit. Shortstop Alex Gonzales committed only his 11th error all year when he dropped a routine ground ball that could have ended the half-inning. Before long, it was Marlins 8, Cubs 3, and Bartman had to be ushered out of the stadium. Florida also won the deciding seventh game of the championship series and went on to defeat the Yankees in the World Series.

CALL　The determining factor in fan interference is the location of the baseball. If the ball is on the playing field side of the wall, then the fielders have the right to make a play and any disruption by a spectator is interference. If the ball is on the spectator side, then the fans can go for the ball—or even go for the player—without the risk of interference.

In the interests of fairness, the rule on fan interference is that umpires impose whatever results would probably have transpired had the interference not taken place. This can be anything—an out, an advance by the runners, or perhaps just a foul ball. Fans in the first few rows must always be aware of the situation so that they do not hurt their team's chances when a live ball comes their way.

Here are the answers:

32. *It is fan interference, and runners are awarded the bases that the umpires judge they would have attained had there been no interference. In this case, the batter was awarded a double and all three base runners were waved home to end the game.*

33. *Because it appeared as though the ball was over the fence when the fan reached for it, the play was ruled no interference—a home run. Replays later showed that the spectator had reached over the playing field, however, and the correct call should have been fan interference—in this case, an out.*

34. *The ball was over the stands, giving the spectators the right to do as they pleased. This is not interference, so the play stood as a foul ball.*

DEFINITION: INTERFERENCE PART 2 (SPECTATOR)

It is spectator's interference (also fan interference) when a spectator reaches onto the field or enters the field and touches a live ball or gets in the way of a player. When a person who is authorized to be on the field (like a security guard or ball boy) gets in the way, then it is only interference if it is intentional.

The Ultimate Penalty

Let's explore the rules that define what is acceptable conduct by both players and their fans.

35. FANS 3, LAW AND ORDER 0

Between games of a doubleheader, the home team decides to provide some on-field entertainment, which quickly leads to a riot that makes the field unplayable.

Question 35: Is the second game postponed or is a forfeit awarded to the visitors?

GAME   In 1979, the Chicago White Sox hosted the Detroit Tigers for a twin bill. The Tigers won the first game, 4–1. Then Comiskey Park became a war zone. It was Disco Demolition Night, a promotion where fans received a discount if they brought along a disco record to burn between

games. When the records went up in smoke, thousands of frenzied disco-haters rushed onto the field. There was a fire in the outfield, destruction of the pitcher's mound, and damage to some of the fences. Detroit earned a 9–0 forfeit victory and a sweep of the doubleheader.

This was not the first or the last misguided baseball promotion that cost the home team the game. In 1974, the Cleveland Indians, hosting the Texas Rangers, staged a dramatic comeback to tie a game at 5–5 with two outs in the bottom of the ninth. With Cleveland on the verge of a miracle victory, hundreds of drunken fans attacked right fielder Jeff Burroughs, and both teams' benches emptied as the players went to rescue him. It was 10-Cent Beer Night in Cleveland, and the 23,134 fans at the stadium were making the most of it. Earlier, in the seventh inning, Texas manager Billy Martin had been forced to evacuate his bullpen, which was close to the rowdiest spectators. During the ninth-inning brawl, umpire Nestor Chylak and Cleveland pitcher Tom Hilgendorf were both hit on the head. The game was forfeited to the Rangers.

A more recent incident occurred in 1995, when the Los Angeles Dodgers gave out promotional baseballs to their fans during a game against the St. Louis Cardinals. Dodger batter Raul Mondesi struck out on a controversial pitch in the bottom of the ninth, with St. Louis leading, 2–1. Both Mondesi and manager Tommy Lasorda were ejected, prompting the fans to throw their baseballs onto the field in protest. After a delay in which the players fled the field for shelter, the fans erupted again with a baseball barrage. The umpires awarded the Cardinals a forfeit victory.

CALL The home team has the responsibility to provide a playable field and safe environment. Any disruption that lasts more than 15 minutes can lead to a forfeit in favor of the visitors. The umpires also have the discretion to terminate a game where they, the players, or the fans may be in danger.

Answer 35: It is a forfeit, and the official score is visitors 9, hosts 0.

36. A SECOND LOOK

After hitting a difficult groundball to the shortstop, the batter thinks he made it safely to first base. But the umpire calls him out. The batter is clearly upset and asks the umpire to check the instant replay.

Question 36: For a change of pace, this question is multiple choice. After the batter asks to check the television replay, should the umpire (a) agree to the request in order to make sure he got the call right, (b) explain that there is no use of instant replay in baseball, or (c) eject the batter from the game?

GAME There were two outs in the bottom of the eighth inning when Pittsburgh Pirate Jack Wilson came to bat against the Arizona Diamondbacks early in the 2003 season. The Pirates were trailing 2–1, giving added importance to every base runner. Diamondback shortstop Tony Womack, moving to his left, fielded Wilson's grounder and fired to first for an unlikely out.

The instant replay, however, seemed to show that Wilson was safe. When he raised this point with umpire Fieldin Culbreth, all he achieved was an early shower. The inning was over, and Arizona held on to win, handing Pittsburgh its eighth loss in nine games.

CALL There is no instant replay in baseball. There are many reasons for this, both practical and philosophical. Purists believe that it is preferable to live with the odd umpire error in judgment rather than sit through countless delays and arguments as fractions of a second are debated over different angles of television footage. It is certainly much more dramatic for fans to witness decisions being made on the field. Plays in baseball are never nullified retrospectively with a yellow flag, as in football, and fans never have to wait patiently for decisions to appear on the scoreboard.

While teams are entitled to file protests over umpires' rules interpretations, there is no higher authority when it comes to judgment calls. In this example, Wilson appealed what he thought was a higher power—television—thereby questioning not only the judgment of the umpire but his authority to make the correct decision. The result was an ejection.

Answer 36: (c) eject the batter from the game.

37. REVENGE

It is a close game between two arch-rivals. In the fifth inning, the visiting pitcher hits a batter. One inning later, the home team's pitcher throws a pitch that hits a visiting batter.

Question 37: What is the automatic penalty when the second batter is hit?

GAME The Minnesota Twins were visiting the Oakland A's early in the 2003 season. Just a few months earlier, the Twins had beaten the A's in a tightly contested five-game divisional playoff series. In the fifth inning on this particular day, Minnesota pitcher Rick Reed plunked Oakland's Ramon Hernandez. Just one inning later, trying to protect a one-run lead, Oakland's Tim Hudson hit Minnesota's Bobby Kielty. Both benches emptied during these two incidents.

The umpires did not believe that Hudson hit Kielty on purpose. The next batter due up was the fence-swinging Torii Hunter, and it seemed unlikely that Hudson would choose to face him with a man on base. The A's went on to win, 4–1.

CALL There is an old tradition in baseball that says that pitchers must "protect their players" by intentionally throwing at players on the opposing team if they think that one of their own players was hit on purpose. Needless to say, this is extremely dangerous because it leads to more players getting hurt, and umpires must do all they can to stamp out this so-called tradition. A lot of progress has been made, but there are many cases where it is difficult to be sure of a pitcher's intent. In the overwhelming majority of cases of a hit batsman in the Major Leagues, the pitcher did not do it on purpose.

In the Twins–A's game, the umpires judged that Hudson was not trying to pitch at Kielty, and they let Hudson stay in the game. This seemed to be the right decision, and no other batters were hit that day.

When an umpire thinks that a pitcher has thrown at a batter on purpose, he should immediately eject that pitcher from the game. Where there is doubt, and if the umpire suspects that someone may try to take revenge, he can issue a warning. A warning can only be made if it is made simultaneously to the pitchers and managers of both teams.

An example of a warning like this took place in a 2005 contest between the Boston Red Sox and the Tampa Bay Devil Rays. By then, these two teams had a five-year history of throwing pitches at each other, and there had been five hit batsmen during the first two games of a three game series. In the third game, Devil Ray pitcher Lance Carter threw behind Red Sox batter Manny Ramirez. Umpire Ted Barrett responded by issuing a warning.

Then the next batter, David Ortiz, dove for the floor to avoid a pitch aimed at his head. As a result, both Carter and manager Lou Piniella were ejected from the game. In the bottom of the inning, Boston pitcher Bronson Arroyo and manager Terry Francona were also ejected when Arroyo threw intentionally at Tampa's Chris Singleton. Boston won that day, 11–3.

It is unfortunate that the penalty for hitting a batter on purpose—the ejection of pitchers and their managers, and sometimes fines and suspensions on top of that—does not dissuade all players from engaging in this reckless behavior. I bet that awarding batters an automatic home run, rather than just first base, would end the problem overnight!

Answer 37: The batter is awarded first base. In cases of a hit batsman, the ejection of the pitcher is only automatic if the umpire believes that he acted intentionally. If a warning has been issued and the act is intentional, then the manager is automatically ejected as well.

38. TRIPPING

In just 1⅓ innings, a starting pitcher issues five walks, hits a batter, and gives up four hits and four runs. Three of the runs scored on bases-loaded walks. This performance inspires the pitching coach to make a trip to the mound. While the coach is out there, he makes a loud comment about the plate umpire's strike zone and is ejected from the game. The team's manager then emerges to try to break up the ensuing argument. While on the field, the manager also speaks to the pitcher.

Question 38: The umpires decide that manager's brief discussion with the pitcher constitutes a second trip to the mound during the same at-bat. Does the pitcher have to leave the game immediately?

GAME Late in the 2000 season, the Chicago Cubs were in a serious slump and would eventually run up a total of 97 losses. When they visited the San Francisco Giants in September, their pitching was in near-total collapse. Pitcher Ruben Quevedo started the day poorly, giving up one run in the first inning and three in the second. Cubs pitching coach Oscar Acosta made a visit to the mound after Quevedo walked Jeff Kent with the bases loaded. Before long, Acosta had been ejected.

The Cubs insisted that despite all of this, they wanted Quevedo to stay in the game. Because the umpires cited manager Don Baylor for a second official visit to the mound during the same at-bat, they made Quevedo leave the game, but not before pitching to the next batter, Ellis Burks. Earlier, in the first inning, Burks had drawn a bases-loaded walk to earn an RBI. Here in the second, he did it again. He would do it one more time, in the sixth inning, earning a total of three runs batted in, despite going hitless that day. The Giants eventually prevailed, 13–2.

CALL Teams are allowed to visit their pitcher on the mound twice during an inning before they are required to bring in a reliever. There is a little-known restriction that limits mound visits to one per batter. A visit to the mound technically begins when a manager or coach crosses the foul lines and ends when he leaves the mound itself. Once leaving the mound, if the manager or coach goes back to talk to the pitcher, it is considered a second official visit.

In these special cases, the pitcher must leave the game, but not before he finishes pitching to the batter who is either about to start or is in the middle of an at-bat. If a manager or coach is warned not to return to the mound for a second, illegal visit, then he will be ejected. In our example, Acosta was responsible for the first visit and Baylor made the second visit, but had not been warned by the umpires. So Baylor was allowed to stay in the game. Acosta and Quevedo, however, had early showers.

Answer 38: No, but he must leave after facing the next batter.

39. HE'S GOT A POINT

The batter hits a hard ground ball that bounces very close to the third base bag and goes to the outfield corner, rolling into foul territory. The third base umpire points toward fair territory, signaling a fair ball. The batter makes it into second base for a double. The third baseman thinks the ball was foul and points to the place just outside the third base bag where he thinks the ball struck the ground.

Question 39: Has the third baseman committed an offense?

GAME This play occurred in 1994, in the seventh inning of the second-longest rain delayed game ever (so long, in fact, that it produced two interesting rule situations—see next question). With many delays and a close score, the tension was high. When Darren Lewis of the visiting Giants hit the ball, umpire Larry Poncino ruled that it bounded past the third base bag in fair territory before going over foul ground. So he judged it a fair ball. Met third baseman Bobby Bonilla tried to show that he thought Poncino was wrong and pointed to a spot on the ground in foul territory where he claimed the ball had bounced. Poncino ejected him for what the rule book calls inciting the crowd. After the game, Bonilla and Met manager Dallas Green told reporters that they did not understand the cause of the ejection.

CALL Baseball probably has the strictest rules in American sports for arguing with officials. Players and managers are expected to argue verbally. Any gesture, such as waving the arms, throwing a hat, kicking dirt, or, in this case, physically pointing out a spot on the ground, can lead to immediate ejection. Bonilla could have stayed in the game if he had told Poncino that he thought the ball bounced in foul territory. But when he pointed to the ground, he signaled to the crowd that he thought the umpire was wrong.

In judging fair/foul decisions on bounding balls near first or third base, it does not necessarily matter where the ball bounced. What matters is where the ball was the very moment when it passed the front edge of the base. So, it is conceivable that the ball bounced in foul territory after passing over the third base bag in the air over fair territory, for a fair ball.

Answer 39: Yes. He incited the crowd and can be ejected from the game.

Popping Out

A simple fly ball to an infielder will bring a smile to a pitcher's face. Sometimes it can also lead to a lot of head-scratching when things get a little more complicated. See if you will be smiling for knowing all the answers or scratching your head, like some of the players in these examples.

The Infield Fly

Look at the following plays and see if you know which ones qualify as an infield fly.

40. CAUGHT

In the bottom of the ninth inning, the home team is trailing, 4–2, but has runners on first and second with two outs. A slugger comes to bat and hits a towering fly ball that stays in the infield.

Question 40: Is it an infield fly, making the game automatically over? The call is on page 109.

GAME In the second-longest rain-delayed game ever recorded, the New York Mets were hosting the San Francisco Giants on a damp Saturday afternoon in 1994. The 1,500 fans who waited the whole seven hours to the bitter end witnessed home runs by the Giants' Matt Williams and Barry Bonds, the two National League home run leaders at the time.

Despite losing Bobby Bonilla in a seventh-inning ejection (see previous question), the Mets seemed like they might pull off a miracle victory in the bottom of the ninth. Hits by Jeromy Burnitz and David Segui put runners on first and second when Jeff Kent came to bat. Kent had hit home runs in his previous at-bat and in the previous game. This time, he was not so successful. He hit a fly ball to the infield off pitcher Rod Beck to end the game. Because there were already two outs, this was not an infield fly.

Mets manager Dallas Green was unlucky enough to have also participated in the longest ever rain-delayed game when he managed the Philadelphia Phillies in 1980. In that game, it took five hours for the rain to clear. The Giants were also the visiting team on that day.

41. BUNTED

In extra innings, the home team has runners on first and second with no outs. Needing just one run to win, the batter tries to advance the runners with a sacrifice bunt. But he executes the bunt poorly and pops out to the catcher.

Question 41: Is this an infield fly or could the catcher have let the ball drop and tried for two outs? The call is on page 109.

GAME In one of the most dramatic playoff games in recent times, the Boston Red Sox, facing elimination, took the New York Yankees to extra innings for the second game in a row. In the 2004 American League Championship Series, the Yankees had taken a 3–0 lead in games. Boston rallied in the fourth game to win on a David Ortiz home run in the 12th inning. In the fifth game, Boston once again came from behind, scoring two runs in the eighth inning to tie the score, 4–4.

The Red Sox opened the bottom of the 11th with singles by Bill Mueller and Mark Belhorn. Johnny Damon then tried a sacrifice bunt to move the runners forward. When he popped out to the catcher for the first out of the half-inning, the umpires did not call an infield fly because it was an attempted bunt rather than a full swing. In any case, the inning ended soon after when Orlando Cabrera grounded into a double play.

The Red Sox finally won the contest in the 14th inning and went on to win the next two games to reach the World Series, where they secured their first championship in 86 years.

42. DROPPED

The bases are loaded with one out when the batter hits a short fly ball. The first baseman cannot hold onto the catch when the second baseman slams into him.

Question 42: Is this an infield fly even though the ball was dropped? The call is on page 109.

GAME This play illustrates how chaos lurks behind every routine play in baseball. Mike Sweeney of the host Kansas City Royals hit a simple pop fly against Kyle Lohse of the Minnesota Twins with one out and the bases loaded early in the 2004 season. First baseman Doug Mientkiewicz appeared to catch the ball when second baseman Michael Cuddyer plowed into him and knocked the ball loose. The umpires had already signaled an infield fly, retiring Sweeney for the second out of the half-inning.

Unsure of whether he was safe or out, Sweeney planted himself on first base. As Desi Relaford tried to score from third, Mientkiewicz gathered up the ball and fired home, but pegged Sweeney in the back. Meanwhile, Royal runner Carlos Beltran took off toward second base where teammate Angel Berroa was standing motionless.

Twins catcher Henry Blanco chased after the ball, now rolling in foul territory, as Beltran headed back toward first base. Blanco then threw to quick-thinking right fielder Jacque Jones, who was covering the bag. Jones tagged Beltran for the third out.

The only remaining question was whether Relaford's run would count. Because there was no force play in effect and because the batter did not make the third out, this was a timing play. Relaford crossed the plate before the third out, so his run stood. This was Kansas City's third and final run in an 8–3 loss to Minnesota.

43. MISSED

The bases are loaded with one out when the batter hits a pop fly in the infield. The ball, which could have been caught, eventually drops to the ground, untouched. A fielder picks the ball up and flips it to the catcher, who is standing on home plate. While the infielders congratulate themselves on an apparent double-play, the runner from third crosses the plate.

Question 43: Is this an infield fly? Is the runner from third out or is he safe at home? The answer is on page 109.

GAME Playing at home in this 2003 contest against the Montreal Expos, San Francisco Giant batter Barry Bonds hit a pop fly that did not make it as far as the pitcher's mound before it fell back to earth. The umpires called it an infield fly, which retired Bonds and removed the force. But a late gust of wind affected the ball, and it hit the ground.

At this point, confusion reigned. When Expo catcher Michael Barrett stepped on the plate with the ball, his action was meaningless because there was no longer a force. Crafty San Francisco runner Neifi Perez acted like he had been put out, but continued to walk home until he touched the plate and the umpire ruled him safe.

By the end of the inning, the Giants had tallied four runs to even the score. The Expos recovered, however, and won, 6–4.

Not one to learn from his mistakes, Barrett did the exact same thing later that year in a game against the Atlanta Braves. Once again thinking that the force remained in effect on the infield fly, Barrett stepped on the plate instead of tagging runner Robert Fick. He then threw to Todd Zeile at third base, where Vinny Castilla arrived safely for the same reason. That day, the Expos were punished for their infield fly illiteracy and lost, 10–6.

44. IN THE OUTFIELD

With runners on first and second and one out, the batter hits a fly ball to short right field. The second baseman appears to settle under it, but at the last second he loses the ball in the sun and then falls over as the ball hits the grass. Once the runners see the second baseman fall, they advance to second and third.

Question 44: Is this an infield fly even though the ball landed in the outfield? The call is on page 109.

GAME In the Washington Nationals' first-ever spring training game in 2005, Washington batter Brendan Harris felt he should have been standing on first base when he advanced teammates Jeffrey Hammonds and Terrmel Sledge on this infield fly. New York Mets second baseman Danny Garcia was charged with an error when both he and the ball fell to earth. The Nationals ended up stranding Hammonds and Sledge, but won the game, 5–3.

CALL The first thing to remember about the infield fly is that the rule is designed to protect the runners. On a routine pop fly that an infielder should be able to catch, it would be unfair if the defense had the option of letting the ball drop in order to record a quick double play. This situation applies when there are fewer than two outs and runners on first and second or first, second, and third. If there are two outs already, then there is no risk of a double play. And if runners are in any other configuration, there is minimal risk of one (considering that the batter should be able to reach first if the pop fly is dropped).

An infield fly does not apply on an attempted bunt, because a bunt is a situation in which the offense no longer deserves protection from a double play. The expected outcome of a bunt with runners on base is one out; it is a sacrifice whose purpose is to advance the lead runners. If the infield fly protected the batting team from a double play on a bunt, then the batter would have nothing to lose by trying.

There is no artificial boundary on an infield fly. The rule has a misleading name, much like a "foul tip" which may be tipped by the batter but is not foul. Similarly, an infield fly can be a fly ball to the outfield. It should more accurately be called an "infielder fly," because the rule states that it applies to a fly ball that can be caught by an infielder (although it may actually be caught by an outfielder or, as in some cases above, not caught at all).

Umpires cannot wait to see if a fielder actually catches the ball before they call an infield fly, because by waiting so long they would not be offering any protection to the runners. The offense may feel victimized by this when the defense commits an error, but this is a judgment call, and it is better for an umpire to call the batter out and prevent an unearned double play than to let chaos break loose. One rule of thumb is to check the runners. If they are running, then it is likely that they do not consider the fly ball to be a routine catch. In the example of the Nationals versus the Mets, the runners waited to see if the ball fell before they advanced. So even though the batter and all runners would have advanced safely on the play, the umpires could not gamble that there would be an error.

On an infield fly, the batter is automatically out, removing the force. Runners can advance if they want, but must tag up if the ball is caught. The ball remains alive.

Here are the answers:

40. *Not an infield fly, because there are already two outs. The game is not over until the ball is caught.*

41. *Not an infield fly. The catcher could have tried to start a double play if he had let the ball drop and then thrown to second or third base.*

42. *Yes, it is an infield fly.*

43. *Yes, it is an infield fly. The runner from third is safe.*

44. *Yes, it is an infield fly.*

45. NO SAFE PLACE TO STAND

Here's a play that is a definite infield fly. With runners on first and second and one out, the batter hits a pop fly toward second base. But the second baseman fails to catch the ball, which strikes the runner who is standing on second. We know that the batter is out on the infield fly, but there is one remaining question:

Question 45: Is the lead runner called out for interference?

GAME In 1997, this rare type of infield fly happened when the Seattle Mariners were visiting the Boston Red Sox. Jay Buhner was on first and Edgar Martinez was on second when Seattle batter Paul Sorrento hit the infield fly straight into Martinez. Not realizing he was protected when on base during an infield fly, Martinez assumed that he too was out when the ball hit him and he walked off the base. Alert Boston shortstop Nomar Garciaparra picked up the ball and tagged Martinez to end the half-inning. Despite the setback, the Mariners won, 5–3.

CALL This is one of those crazy plays that was not covered by the rule book until it actually happened. Legend has it that Al Somers, the author of the apparent "fourth out" (see Question 21), was the first umpire to face this situation. Somers ruled that because the infield fly is designed to protect the runners by allowing them to stay on their bases without the threat of a force out, it would be unfair for those runners to be called out for interference while remaining on base.

Normally, runners are out for interference when a hit ball (ground ball or fly ball) strikes them before passing an infielder. This applies even when the runners are on base. In short, the fielders have first rights to a batted ball, and runners must get out of the way or risk being called out for interference. The only exception is during an infield fly.

Answer 45: No.

Weirdness is Catching

Here are some unusual plays involving catchers. Let's see if you can figure out the correct call.

46. A SWING AND A NICK

The bases are loaded with one out when the batter hits a ground ball to the pitcher. But on the swing, his bat nicked the catcher's mitt.

Question 46: Because his swing touched the catcher's mitt, does the batter get another chance to hit?

GAME Playing in Cincinnati, the Milwaukee Brewers loaded the bases in the third inning of a scoreless contest in 2004. Pitcher Jimmy Haynes of the Reds thought he had pitched his way out of trouble when his offering to Craig Counsell

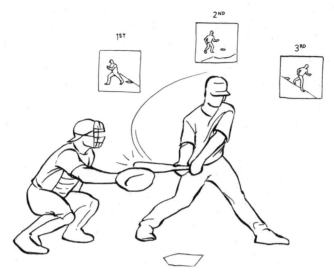

came back to him for a possible double play to end the half-inning. But when Counsell's bat touched catcher Javier Valentin's mitt, it became a case of catcher's interference.

Counsell was awarded first base, forcing home Wes Helms from third. This made the score 1–0. The Brewers' rally continued with an RBI single by Keith Ginter. Soon, Lyle Overbay hit a grand slam to make the score 6–0. The Brewers held on to win, 6–2, all thanks to the interference play that kept the Brewers' rally alive.

CALL Whenever the catcher's mitt touches a bat during a swing, it is catcher's interference. In most cases, the batter is awarded first base. It is a delayed dead ball, so that if the batter gets a hit on the play and the other runners advance, then the play will proceed as if no interference took place. In some cases, the offensive manager may elect to decline the interference call. For example, if on a catcher's interference play the batter hits a sacrifice fly that scores a run, the batting team might prefer to keep the run and the out rather than have the batter go to first base and the other runner return to third.

Answer 46: No. The batter is awarded first base.

DEFINITION: INTERFERENCE PART 3 (CATCHER)

It is *catcher's interference* (also *defensive interference*) when a fielder (usually the catcher) impedes a batter attempting to hit a pitch.

Who's Out?

There are a number of reasons why a catcher may be impeded from throwing out a runner trying to steal a base. Depending on the cause of the interference, there may be different outcomes. Here are two cases.

47. BEAN BALL

There is one out, a runner on first, and a full count on the batter. On the pitch, the runner takes off for second base. It is a swinging strikeout, and the catcher attempts to throw out the runner going for second. On his throw, the catcher's arm nicks the umpire's face mask. When he releases the ball, it hits the batter in the head. The ball then bounces off of the batter's helmet and into left field, and the runner reaches third base.

Question 47: Does the runner get to stay on third, is he sent back to first, or is he out for possible interference by his teammate? The call is on page 118.

GAME In 2005, the New York Yankees were visiting the Toronto Blue Jays when Blue Jay batter Frank Catalanotto struck out swinging. With Russ Adams stealing second, Catalanotto's momentum carried his head into the path of catcher Jorge Posada's throw, and the ball deflected into the outfield.

Posada's arm, however, clipped the umpire, making it a case of umpire's interference. The ball was dead, and

Adams was sent back to first base. The Yankees eventually won, 11–2.

48. BIG SWING

With no outs and a runner on first base, the batter swings and misses for strike three as the runner tries to steal second. The batter's backswing hits the catcher, who is unable to throw to second base to try to retire the runner.

Question 48: Does the runner get to stay at second, is he sent back to first, or is he out for possible interference by his teammate? The call is on page 118.

GAME The day after the Frank Catalanotto interference play, Russ Adams was again involved in this slightly different play, which had the identical result of preventing Jorge Posada's throw to second base. When striking out against Yankee relief pitcher Tom Gordon in the eighth inning, Adams's bat continued around and hit Posada on the backswing. Posada was unable to throw to second base on a steal attempt by Blue Jay Orlando Hudson. Hudson was returned to first base, but no outs were charged on this unintentional interference. The Yankees held on to win again, this time by the much slimmer margin of 4–3.

Days after Posada was twice victimized by these interference plays, he committed catcher's interference when he got in the way of a swing by Darin Erstad of the now-cumbersomely named Los Angeles Angels of Anaheim. It seems that where Posada goes, interference follows.

CALL The deflection off Catalanotto is fairly straightforward: The umpire interfered with the catcher's throw, and so the runner was returned to his original base. On the Adams strikeout, the same result applied because the interference happened on the backswing. Both plays bring up some intriguing possibilities had events unfolded slightly differently.

On either play, if Posada had been able to throw out the runner at second base despite the interference, then the out would still count on the assumption that it was not really interference after all. For this reason, it is a delayed dead ball.

The umpire's interference seemed to negate apparent batter's interference by Catalanotto. Had the umpire not gotten in the way and had Catalanotto intentionally interfered with the throw, then the runner would have been called out. What if Catalanotto had *not* struck out *and* intentionally interfered? In this case, the batter would be out and the runner sent back to his original base.

In a case of interference on a batter's backswing, as happened with Adams, then no out is charged and runners must return to their bases.

When the offense is guilty of interference, at least one person will be called out (except when the interference happens on the backswing). When the umpire causes interference, then no one is out.

Here are the answers:

47. *It is umpire's interference, and the runner must return to first base.*

48. *It is a case of offensive interference in which no one is called out, and the runner must return to first base.*

DEFINITION: INTERFERENCE PART 4 (UMPIRE)

It is *umpire's interference* when the umpire gets in the way of a catcher trying to prevent a stolen base *or* when a fair batted ball hits an umpire before touching the pitcher or passing an infielder (not including the pitcher).

---

49. UNMASKED

The score is tied in an extra-inning game, and the potential winning run for the home team is just 90 feet away on third base. The pitch comes in low, hitting the dirt. The batter swings and misses, and the ball bounces a few feet away from the catcher. Sensing a chance to win the game, the runner from third breaks for the plate. The catcher scoops up the ball with his mask and then applies the tag with the ball in his hand before the runner is able to score.

Question 49: Is this a legal play by the catcher?

GAME In this play, Mitch Webster of the Los Angeles Dodgers was batting against Jeff McCurry of the Pittsburgh Pirates in 1995, and the game was tied, 10–10. The game was truly remarkable, with 39 hits between both teams and yet no home runs. In the 10th inning, both sides had rallied for three runs, sending the marathon contest to the 11th. In the bottom of the 11th, when McCurry's pitch hit the dirt, rookie catcher Angelo Encarnacion used his mask to grab the ball before he made the tag. The umpires ruled this to be an illegal use of equipment and awarded all base runners one base. This meant that instead of being out, the runner from third scored the winning run. Encarnacion was charged with the error that cost his team the game.

Encarnacion would probably like to forget this embarrassing moment from his brief Major League career. He made amends five days later, however, when he hit a rare inside-the-park home run in a victory over the Florida Marlins.

CALL Part of the notion of fairness in baseball is that equipment should only be used for the purposes for which it is designed. Gloves and mitts are there to help players catch the ball. Masks protect catchers from being hit in the face. Hats are used to shade the eyes from the sun or stadium lights. The rule book specifies penalties for illegal use of equipment in order to prevent the defense from gaining an unfair advantage.

On a batted ball, if a defensive player takes off his hat to stop the ball or throws his glove to deflect the ball, the award is three bases—an automatic triple. This is one reason you never see outfielders throwing their gloves at balls they cannot reach. If a violation occurs (and equipment must actually touch the ball—there is no penalty for throwing a glove at the ball and missing), the ball remains alive, so the batter is able to try to score if he wants to risk it. If an outfielder throws his glove and stops a ball from passing over the fence for a home run, then the home run is awarded.

In the 1992 movie *A League of Their Own*, Madonna stars as center fielder Mae Mordabito, who tries to impress the crowd by catching a routine pop fly with her hat. If this were real baseball instead of a movie, then this play would not have been ruled an out, but would have been an automatic triple. (Hollywood take note: The author is available as a rules consultant for forthcoming movies, especially those starring female pop icons!)

On a thrown ball where a fielder commits a similar violation, the award is two bases. The rule book does not actually mention pitched balls, however, which was what Encarnacion picked up with his mask. But the same logic applies. Here, the umpires reasoned by analogy with balls that go out of play: On a thrown ball that rolls out of play, the award is two bases; on a pitched ball that leaves the playing field, the award is one base. They concluded that illegal use of equipment on a pitched ball should also lead to a one-base award.

The umpires' quick thinking in this strange play shows that it is not enough for the men-in-blue to know the rule book. They need to understand the theory behind the rules, so that they can be prepared to make judgments on situations that may not yet be covered by the book.

Answer 49: No. It is an illegal use of equipment, and all base runners are awarded one base.

50. STRAY FOOT

The lead-off man for the visiting team begins a game with a base hit. The pitcher then gets two quick strikes on the next batter. Expecting a "waste pitch," the catcher lines up on the outside corner of the plate, with his foot slightly outside of the 43-inch catcher's box as the next pitch is delivered for a ball.

Question 50: What is the penalty, if any, for the catcher's stray foot? What is the count?

GAME In the 2000 season, Ron Belliard of the Milwaukee Brewers got an infield single to start things off against Greg

Maddux of the Atlanta Braves. With the count 0–2 against Marquis Grissom, rookie catcher Fernando Lunar placed his right foot outside of the catcher's box. Umpire John Shulock called a balk and then ejected Braves manager Bobby Cox during the ensuing argument.

Belliard later scored on a fielder's choice, but he probably would not have done so if it weren't for the balk. A home run by Jeromy Burnitz in the fourth inning proved to be enough to give Milwaukee a 2–1 win, despite Maddux pitching a complete game.

Lunar later complained that the catcher's box seemed smaller that day. Controversially, the Braves' own television announcers argued that the team's groundskeepers had been painting the catcher's box too wide. Brewers manager Davey Lopes complained during the previous game, and the box seemed to shrink back down to regulation size for the game that Maddux started. If the catcher's box really was smaller that day, then no one told Lunar!

CALL Catchers must position themselves with both feet in the catcher's box as pitches are delivered. The penalty for straying out of the box is a balk, meaning that all base runners get a free pass to the next base. This rarely happens, and when it does, it is usually during an intentional walk. The balk on Maddux's 0–2 pitch was an extremely rare example of this kind of play, and umpires have come to expect that an argument with the manager tends to follow rare events. Manager Bobby Cox would hesitate, however, to blame the umpires for another rare event that happened that day: Burnitz's 454-foot home run was the longest in the history of Turner Field.

Answer 50: It is a balk, and the runner is awarded second base. The count remains 0–2.

Home at Last

The home run might be the most awesome play in baseball. Yet the term *home run* is not defined in the rule book and does not even appear in the index. Instead, it is covered by a number of different rules that, separately, govern batters and runners, and are mutually contradictory and incomplete. Perhaps for this reason, there are all sorts of confusing situations that can arise when the ball takes a few detours before going over the fence and when the batter does strange things on the way home.

51. A STAR IS BORN

In the eighth inning of an interleague game, the home team is winning 3–1 and has a runner on base when an untested rookie steps to the plate. The batter hits the ball deep to left field. Uncertain where it will land, he runs quickly around the bases, finally scoring before he realizes that the ball had cleared the fence on a fly in fair territory.

Question 51: Is this a home run?

GAME Well, obviously this is a home run, so consider this a bonus question. On June 15, 2005, 23-year-old Seattle Mariner rookie Mike Morse hit his first Major League home run. He did it against Ryan Madson of the Philadelphia Phillies and helped the Mariners on their way to a 5–1 victory. I just wanted to use this opportunity to congratulate Morse and wish him all the best for a long and productive career in the Majors. I will be sending a signed copy of this book to him in the hope that he might return the gesture by sending a signed picture of himself to me (c/o the publisher).

Mike, I'm sure you'll be a superstar. Just remember to be nice to the umpires.

CALL You think all the home run questions will be this easy. Think again.

Answer 51: Yes.

52. PREMATURE CELEBRATION

The score is tied, 3–3, in extra innings when the home team loads the bases with one out. The batter hits an apparent grand slam home run over the fence, but is so excited that he and the runner from first base stop in their tracks and celebrate together. The rest of the team joins them, and the two runners never complete the trip around the bases. Meanwhile, the runners from second and third have gone around to score.

Question 52: Is this a home run and what is the final score of the game?

GAME This intriguing play was one of the greatest post-season comebacks in the history of the New York Mets— a team that has won its share of exciting October games. Trailing 3–2 against the visiting Atlanta Braves in the bottom of the 15th inning of Game 5 of the 1999 National League Championship Series, the Mets put together a dramatic rally. With the help of a lead-off single by Shawon Dunston and walks by Matt Franco, John Olerud, and Todd Pratt, New York had tied the score and loaded the bases.

Needing no more than a base hit or sacrifice fly to win the game, batter Robin Ventura hit a Kevin McGlinchy pitch over the fence. Pinch-runner Roger Cedeno scored from third, Olerud scored from second, and Ventura and Pratt both stopped around second base to celebrate. The game ended with the score 4–3 on this memorable "grand slam single." The last laugh went to the Braves, however, who won the next game and advanced to the World Series.

CALL Normally, in the bottom of the ninth or in extra innings, a game is over the moment the home team takes the lead. The exception to this is a game-ending home run, when all runners are permitted to score even if preceding runners have already taken the lead and effectively settled the outcome of the game. Had Pratt and Ventura continued around the bases, completing the home run, then the final score would have been 7–3. As it was, the fact that Ventura did not score meant that the play was not a home run, and so the game ended the moment the Mets took the lead, when Cedeno scored.

During the play, Ventura could have been called out for two separate reasons, either for passing Pratt or for abandoning his effort around the bases. Pratt could also have been called out for not continuing to run. The intriguing aspect of this play is that the Mets scored the go-ahead run and the third out was recorded (if we consider both Ventura and Pratt to have been out). In an apparent paradox, the game was over when Cedeno crossed the plate, but the game could have continued were it not for the fact that Ventura and Pratt abandoned their efforts. In effect, Olerud's run was withdrawn.

Matters could have become very thorny had either Ventura or Pratt failed to advance at least one base on the play. For example, if Pratt had stopped running and begun his celebrations before touching second base, then his out would have been a force out, and no run can score when the third out is a force out. Cedeno's run would not have counted, and the game might still be going on today. It would have taken a very brave umpire to nullify a game-winning grand slam in the playoffs over a technicality, but the Mets took an unnecessary risk when two runners abandoned their efforts around the basepaths.

There was a similar play in 2005, when the Milwaukee Brewers defeated the Cincinnati Reds, 6–5, in the bottom of the ninth on an apparent ground-rule double that bounced over the outfield wall. With the score tied and the bases loaded with no outs, Damian Miller hit a ball that hit the ground and continued into the outfield bleachers. Carlos Lee scored the winning run from third. Lyle Overbay did not bother to run all the way home from second. But even if he had, it would not have counted since the game was already over. Miller's hit was scored as a single.

Answer 52: Not a home run. The final score is 4–3.

53. BACK TO HOME

After a batter hits the ball over the fence for a home run, he runs to first base, but then turns around and jogs the rest of the way around the bases facing backward.

Question 53: Is this allowed?

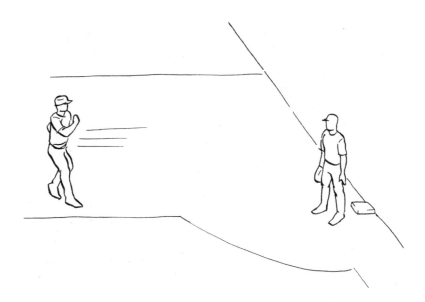

GAME Jimmy Piersall of the 1963 New York Mets had a mental illness that, by his own admission, made him more famous than did his mediocre baseball abilities. His agonizing career was portrayed by *Psycho*-star Anthony Perkins in the 1957 movie *Fear Strikes Out*. Before the construction of

Shea Stadium, the Mets played their home games in the Polo Grounds, which had very short fences down the line. Piersall's homer—his first in two years and the 100th of his career—traveled a mere 258 feet. Since 1959, all *new* Major League ballparks must have fences at least 325 feet from home plate. But for the older parks, according to the rule book, a fair ball hit over a fence at least 250 feet away is a home run.

For no good reason, Piersall ran most of the way around the bases with his rear leading the way. Despite the annoyance of the Philadelphia Phillies pitcher Dallas Green, there is nothing illegal about his play. The home run counted. Piersall's strange display did not go unpunished, however. Two days later, the Mets released him.

CALL If a player runs around the bases clockwise in order to confuse the defense or to mock the game, then umpires will immediately call him out. But there is nothing in the rule book that says you must face forward when running the bases.

Answer 53: Yes, but it looks silly.

Going, going ... huh?

Let's see if you can determine if the ruling is home run or not in the following situations.

54. OFF A FIELDER

When an outfielder tries to catch a long fly ball, he mistimes his jump and the ball bounces off his head and over the fence.

Question 54: Is this a home run? The call is on page 144.

GAME The unlucky outfielder in this case was Jose Canseco, playing for the Texas Rangers in 1993. His outfield miscue gifted a home run to Cleveland Indian batter Carlos

Martinez. Inevitably, the Indians won by a single run, 7–6. The blow seemed to have impaired Canseco's judgment because three days later he had the funny idea to *pitch* during a one-sided loss to the Boston Red Sox. Pitching a full inning soon led to elbow surgery, and the next year Canseco abandoned the outfield altogether and became a designated hitter. He was soon traded to the Red Sox, presumably not for his pitching or fielding abilities.

In a similar but less painful play in 2004, Philadelphia Phillies outfielder Jason Michaels was generous in helping a ball over the fence for a home run. Charles Thomas of the Atlanta Braves hit a deep fly ball that Michaels juggled twice before unintentionally flipping it into the hands of a spectator. Thomas's unexpected four-bagger did not affect the outcome of the game, which the Phillies won, 9–4.

55. ON A RICOCHET

In a stadium with an awkward outfield fence that has a window for pitchers in the bullpen to watch the action and that creates funny angles, a long fly ball hits a windowsill below the yellow line that marks the top of the fence. Then, without hitting the ground, the ball ricochets over a different part of the fence and lands in the stands in fair territory.

Question 55: Is this a home run? The call is on page 144.

GAME The visiting Tampa Bay Devil Rays struggled with the stadium dimensions and with the host Texas Rangers when they dropped three straight games in 2003. Devil Ray batter Javier Valentin hit what both he and manager Lou Piniella thought was a home run when the ball bounced off a windowsill on the outfield fence and then landed in the crowd without hitting the ground. But the umpires had other ideas and awarded a double.

It did not really matter, however, because Valentin scored on the next play when Jared Sandberg hit a double that knocked him home. This gave Tampa a 3–1 lead. In the bottom of the inning, however, Texas scored seven times and went on to win, 10–8.

56. ON A BOUNCE

After leading by as much as 6–0, the home team suffers a major collapse and falls behind, 8–6. They manage to pull back within one run, and the score is 8–7 in the bottom of the ninth. With two runners on and no one out, the batter hits a long fly ball that hits the top of the fence before continuing into the stands.

Question 56: Is this a home run? The call is on page 144.

GAME Marquis Grissom of the San Francisco Giants was the hero in this rollercoaster of a game against the visiting Colorado Rockies in 2005. With Pedro Feliz and Edgardo Alfonzo on base, Grissom crushed a pitch by Colorado reliever Scott Dohmann to the top of the wall. When it then bounced over, it became a home run, propelling San Francisco to a 10–8 victory.

57. BOUNCE TO A FAN

A batter's long fly ball hits the top of the fence and then goes straight up in the air. It appears likely that it will land back on the playing field when a fan reaches out to catch it. The fan deflects the ball but fails to hold on, and it falls to the grass.

Question 57: Is this a home run? The call is on page 144.

GAME Marquis Grissom's first month of the 2005 season for the San Francisco Giants featured two hits off the top of the fence during games against the Colorado Rockies. A week after his game-winning blast mentioned in the previous example, Grissom hit another one. This time, the ball did not go over but came about as close as possible to doing so before the fan interfered. The umpires called it a double. During the very next inning, Grissom hit a home run that cleared the fence in the normal fashion. The Giants won again, this time 13–6.

58. PINBALL

With a runner on first and no one out, the batter hits a deep fly ball to center field. The ball bounces off the top of the wall, rebounds back onto the forehead of a surprised center-fielder, and then ricochets over the fence.

Question 58: Is this a home run? The call is on page 144.

GAME In this extremely rare and somewhat painful play in 1977, Warren Cromartie of the host Montreal Expos was at bat and Rick Monday of the Los Angeles Dodgers was the unlucky outfielder. When Monday deflected the ball into the crowd in fair territory, the umpires called a ground-rule double, sending runner Tony Perez to third and Cromartie to second. Perez soon scored the game-tying run in the Expos' come-from-behind 4–3 victory.

59. CAUGHT

A batter hits a deep fly ball to right field. The right fielder leaps in the air and catches it, but his momentum carries him over the fence while in possession of the ball.

Question 59: Is this a home run? The call is on page 144.

GAME Fenway Park in Boston has a very low fence between right field and the bullpen, and it has been the scene of a number of outfielders tumbling out of the playing field.

In 1997, Jay Buhner of the Seattle Mariners robbed Scott Hatteberg of the Boston Red Sox of a home run when he made a spectacular catch while falling over the outfield fence. The play, which made little difference in the Mariners' 4–0 loss, aggravated a bad knee, and Buhner soon had to have surgery.

In 2003, Bobby Kielty of the Toronto Blue Jays tumbled over the same fence when he caught a blast by Boston's Trot Nixon. The Red Sox scored plenty of runs in other ways that day and won, 9–4.

In both of these cases, there were no runners on base. But had there been base runners, then they would each have been awarded one base.

60. CAUGHT ON A RICOCHET

The scoreThis play is clearly not a home run, but it is useful to consider along with the other examples. The batter hits a long fly ball to the warning track. The outfielder gets to it just in time, but bobbles the ball. Eventually, the ball rebounds off the fence and, without hitting the ground, is finally caught.

Question 60: Is this a legal catch? The call is on page 144.

GAME In this incident in 1999, New York Yankee Derek Jeter was the batter and Baltimore Oriole Albert Belle was the ball-bobbling right fielder. Jeter wound up with a double that never touched the ground.

CALL What is a home run? It seems an obvious question at first. A batted ball that flies over the fence without hitting the ground is a home run.

If the ball hits the ground before going over the fence, then it is a "ground-rule double" (not because it is a "ground rule" but because it is the rule for a ball that hits the *ground*; no stadium can create a "ground rule" that awards more or less than two bases on this play).

But what if the ball hits some combination of outfielder and outfield wall before going over? Here's where the rule gets interesting. The home run is governed by two separate rules, one for batters and one for runners. But first we need to understand some terms: A "bounding" ball is a ball that has hit the ground or the fence or something other than a defensive player; this contrasts with a ball "in flight" which has not hit anything, except possibly a fielder.

The rule that governs batters says that a home run is granted on a batted ball that goes over the fence without *bouncing on the ground*. The rule goes on to state that when a ball is *deflected* by a fielder over the fence in fair territory, it is a home run unless it is a bounding ball. This rule does not say anything about a bounding ball that goes over the fence without being deflected by a fielder. In contrast to this wording, the rule for runners states that a home run occurs when a ball goes over the fence in flight. Now let's apply these rules to our examples.

Martinez's blast that hit Canseco on the head was a home run by both rules. It was a home run for the runners because it was in flight. It was a home run for the batter because it was deflected by a fielder over the fence and it was not a bounding ball.

Cromartie's blast, which first hit the fence, then hit Monday, and then went over, is a ground-rule double by both rules. Because it hit the wall, it was no longer in flight, making it a double for the runners. And because it was a bounding ball that deflected off a fielder, it was a double for the batter.

Valentin's blast that hit the windowsill on the fence is a ground-rule double by the rule that governs runners because it was not in flight. But it seems to be a home run by the rule that governs batters because it did not bounce on the ground and was not deflected by a fielder. In this case, the umpires ruled it a double, perhaps because the rule on batters does not specifically address this situation, while the rule on runners does. Also, the rule that covers runners is written in more general language and applies to batters as well, in their capacity as runners once they have hit the ball. In any case, it would be unthinkable to allow the batter to round the bases while only allowing the runners to advance two bases.

Now things get more confusing. Grissom's game-winning hit off the top of the fence is indistinguishable from Valentin's, at least according to the rule book. It should have been a home run for the batter because it did not bounce on the ground and was not deflected by a fielder. But because it hit the fence before going over, it was not in flight, so it should have been a double for the runners. So why was this a home run, but Valentin's hit wasn't?

Here, common sense takes over where the rule book lets us down. It seems that if a ball hits the top of the fence, then everything depends on where it goes next. If it goes over, then the umpires consider that in a sense it was already a home run when it stopped being in flight. If it comes back onto the field, as in Grissom's double, then it is not a home run.

But Valentin's hit also made it over the fence. Where, exactly, is the top of the fence for the purposes of this interpretation? The stadium design in Texas helped in this case, because the windowsill was clearly below a big yellow line on the fence. And, intuitively we can see why Valentin did not deserve a home run, while Grissom did. Of course, Martinez did not deserve a home run either, but Canseco's bone-headed play ensured that his hit was a home run.

Moving on, both Jay Buhner and Bobby Kielty made legal catches before leaving the field of play. Therefore, the outs counted even though they fell over the outfield wall.

I included Albert Belle's catch in order to illustrate the idea of a ball being "in flight." When a ball is no longer in flight, because it has hit the ground or a fence, then it can no longer be a home run and can no longer be caught for an out.

Are we clear so far? Here are some hypothetical situations that caused me to lose some sleep: What if an outfielder jumps to the top of the wall and reaches over to glove a ball that has deflected off the top of the wall and is headed into the crowd? Is it a home run already? Is it in flight? Is it a catch?

In all probability, this would be considered a base hit rather than a catch and the ball would remain in play. But it is no different from Grissom's home run, which must have been in flight by the logic of the home run rule that covers runners. If a ball is in flight, then it can be also caught for an out. How could Grissom's home run be in flight after it hit the top of the wall, but this hypothetical hit would no longer be in flight, just because a fielder was there to catch it?

Like in quantum mechanics, where subatomic particles can appear to be in two places at once, a hit off the top of the wall is simultaneously in flight and not in flight, and only settles into one or the other state of existence when it hits something else. If it continues into the crowd, then it is in flight and is a home run. If a fielder catches it, then it is not in flight and is not a catch.

Now, let's add a further twist. Let us say a fly ball bounces on the top of the fence and is continuing on its way over the fence, when an outfielder jumps up, grabs the ball in his glove, and falls into the crowd. Here we have a ball that is not in flight and therefore not caught for an out, but which is fielded by a player going into a dead ball area. My interpretation would be to treat this like an overthrow and award all runners two bases from the moment the outfielder falls over the wall. (It is not a one-base award as in Question 1, because that only applies to balls that are caught before the fielder falls out of play.)

Perhaps in addition to managers, each team should have a lawyer or a scientist in uniform in the dugout. Just try to remember that baseball is only a game, and, like back-yard stickball, its rules must be updated to account for every unexpected situation that comes along.

Here are the answers:

54. *Home run.*

55. *Not a home run. A ground-rule double.*

56. *Home run.*

57. *Fan interference, ruled a double.*

58. *Not a home run. A ground-rule double.*

59. *Not a home run. A legal catch.*

60. *Not a catch.*

DEFINITION: HOME RUN

A *home run* is a base hit in which the batter legally advances to home plate. The batter is awarded a home run when his batted ball, without hitting the ground, fence, or any object other than a fielder, passes over the fence in fair territory. *Exception*: if the ball hits the top of the fence, carries over on its own accord, and is not fielded by a defensive player, then it is also a home run.

Scoreboard

How many questions did you get right? Remember to be honest, like a good umpire. No partial credit is given on questions that ask for more than one rule (sorry, but no one ever gives umpires a break for being half right).

60: Congratulations, you are a World Series umpire crew chief!

50–59: Major Leaguer

40–49: Minor Leaguer

30–39: Little Leaguer

20–29: Microscopic Leaguer

10–19: Only casually acquainted with bat-and-ball sports

5–9: You think a "baseball diamond" is a fashion accessory

0–4: Congratulations, you are a Major League player, manager, or broadcaster!

Index

About the Author

Michael A. Morse spent much of the 1980s and early 1990s in the right field bleachers of Yankee Stadium. Suspecting that he might be bad luck for the team, he moved to England before the 1996 season.

Michael trained at the Harry Wendelstedt School for Umpires, where he scored poorly in virtually every umpiring category except for knowledge of the rules, where he was one of the best in the class, rivaling some future Major Leaguers.

Michael umpired amateur baseball in New York and Chicago before making it to the National League . . . . of Great Britain. He is also an umpire in the Confédération Européene de Baseball. Off the field, he has a Ph.D. in the history of science and works as a fundraiser.